MONASTIC WISDOM SERIES: NUMBER TWENTY-SIX

Francis Acharya, ocso

Cistercian Spirituality

An Ashram Perspective

MONASTIC WISDOM SERIES: NUMBER TWENTY-SIX

Cistercian Spirituality
An Ashram Perspective

by

Francis Acharya, ocso

Edited with an Introduction by
Michael Casey, ocso

𝛂

Cistercian Publications
www.cistercianpublications.org

LITURGICAL PRESS
Collegeville, Minnesota
www.litpress.org

A Cistercian Publications title published by Liturgical Press

Cistercian Publications
Editorial Offices
Abbey of Gethsemani
3642 Monks Road
Trappist, Kentucky 40051
www.cistercianpublications.org

1   2   3   4   5   6   7   8   9

Library of Congress Cataloging-in-Publication Data

Acharya, Francis.
    Cistercian spirituality : an Ashram perspective / by Francis Acharya; edited with an introduction by Michael Casey.
        p. cm.
    ISBN 978-0-87907-026-7 — ISBN 978-0-87907-900-0 (e-book)
    1. Cistercians—India.   2. Monastic and religious life—India.   I. Casey, Michael, 1942–   II. Title.

BX3403.A24 2011
255'.120954--dc22   2010036916

O MONK!

Do not harbor any illusion about the quality of your life.
Your charism will not flourish or shine simply
by keeping the rules and prescriptions printed in books,
nor will your life be deepened by irresponsibility or
the shallowness of hazardous innovations.

The true strength of the monastic charism
is to be sought in your openness to renunciation,
to personal enjoyment of quiet and silence,
in your love of prayer, both personal and in community,
to realize the value of the Cross in your life!

The genuine renewal which it should bring about
is the growth of your life in Jesus and His life in you,
with docility to His Spirit.
The growth of your life in Him,
must be sought at the source of life:
the Cross and the Resurrection of Jesus.

CONTENTS

PART TWO:
THE SCHOOL OF THE LORD'S SERVICE LEADING
TO PERFECT LOVE

INTRODUCTION

The life of Abbot Francis Mahieu Acharya (1912–2002) is already well known from the excellent biography written by his niece, a year before his death.[1] At the age of twenty-three he entered the Cistercian abbey of Scourmont in his native Belgium. For twenty years he lived as a Strict Observance Cistercian before setting out for India in 1955 with the intention of founding an Indian-style monastery. In 1958, accompanied by Fr. Bede Griffiths, OSB, he moved to Kurisumala in the southern Indian state of Kerala. Here, on the Mountain of the Cross, he built his Cistercian Ashram; instituted a way of life that combined Cistercian, West-Syrian Christian and Indian traditions; and formed disciples by his profound teaching and commonsense judgment.

In more ways than one the ashram was a *sui generis* monastery, quite unlike anything else then existing in the Church. It was practically independent, coming loosely under the authority of the local Syro-Malankara bishop and the Vatican Congregation for the Oriental Churches. Fr. Francis reveled in the freedom of his situation and was able to fine-tune the monastic lifestyle without outside interference. When, however, he reached the age of eighty and various health problems made thoughts of his mortality unavoidable, he began to be concerned about the future leadership of the ashram.

At this time he started making inquiries about the possibility of aggregating his monastery to the Order in which he himself

---

1. Marthe Mahieu-De Praetere, *Kurisumala: Francis Mahieu Acharya: A Pioneer of Christian Monasticism in India*, Cistercian Studies 214 (Kalamazoo: Cistercian Publications, 2007).

had been formed. A first step was to begin negotiations with the abbot of Scourmont, his own former monastery, who visited the ashram in 1993. He was followed, in the next year, by Abbot General Bernardo Olivera. After the favorable vote of the General Chapter of 1996, the formal process of incorporation was initiated, which included the provision that a monk of the Order would spend time with the community, helping it to realign its vision of monastic life to harmonize with the spirit of the Order it was about to join.

During 1997 and 1998 I spent a fair amount of time at Kurisumala, spaced over several visits. My first task was to review with the community the foundational Cistercian texts of the twelfth century with a view to appreciating their essential values and the ways in which they were practically expressed. At that time I had the very strong impression that Kurisumala was already profoundly Cistercian in spirit and in practice and that, in many ways, the manner in which the monks lived their monastic life was much closer to the primitive observance than what could be observed in many established monasteries of the Order. Over the years this impression strengthened. It was my judgment that Fr. Francis's community was already deeply imbued with the Cistercian charism and that a long period of transition and preparation was not necessary. This conclusion was subsequently confirmed by two visiting abbots and July 9, 1998, was set as the date for the ceremony of affiliation.

The ashram was now raised to the status of an abbey and pastorally supported through the structures of the Order, but the question of succession remained urgent. Although he had earlier strongly resisted the idea of codifying ashram practice, Fr. Francis now became convinced that it was necessary to have some form of spiritual directory for the ongoing guidance of his community—an updated and inculturated version of the nineteenth-century volumes he had known in his early days at Scourmont.

And so, already in his late eighties, Fr. Francis began work. Although his library at Kurisumala was relatively small, he was not without resources—and he was helped in his task by a good memory, a systematic approach and a synthetic mind. Before he came to India, he had received an excellent monastic formation under Dom Anselme Le Bail at Scourmont; he had studied at Rome and Paris, served as Master of Novices at Caldey, was a keen reader in many languages and a lifelong student. He had more than sixty years of varied monastic experience and he was a spiritually literate man with sound and balanced judgment. With a vigor typical of him, but still surprising in a man of his age, he sought to bring together in compact form not only the fruits of many years of study, but also to shape it according to the spirit that he desired to impart to his monks at Kurisumala.

Father Francis wrote as he spoke. At heart there was a contemplative fascination with the mysterious depths of God and great appreciation of the quasi-sacramental channels by which, over the course of a lifetime, the grace of God softens the heart and increases the pace of conversion. He was in no doubt about the efficacy of the monastic observances in providing an environment in which this transformation or deification occurs, and he was quite shrewd in identifying ways in which a monk might seek to escape its rigor. He was not a harsh man but he could be a stern master, bluntly pointing out delusions and evasions and not afraid to insist on greater effort. His writing is possessed of this same dual character: a mystical elevation alternating with a down-to-earth realism.

The book he produced at this time was a simple photocopied edition, continually revised and corrected, with many inserts and interpolations. Father Francis was exigent in his desire to get things just right and was always seeking to improve his text, using whatever materials daily Providence arranged. Having heard the result read at meals during my stays at Kurisumala, it seemed to me that his work would be helpful for a wider readership. Although it is written mindful of the specific customs and conditions of Kurisumala, it stands up well as a clear exposition of monastic tradition from a Cistercian viewpoint, enhanced as it often is with the experiential wisdom Fr. Francis gleaned during a long monastic lifetime.

In editing the text I have attempted to make Fr. Francis's own voice as audible as I could. I have removed some of the supplementary material that he had later included. Often this impeded the smooth passage of his ideas without adding anything substantial to his presentation. I have not attempted to identify the sources from which he drew his content, but I have been aware that often he was summarizing or paraphrasing part of a book or article, without bothering with footnotes. He was more concerned with the final product than with its ingredients. Indeed, once or twice I have been flattered to have some of my own words recycled.

This book is offered to a wider world in the hope that it will serve as a means of making and deepening contact with the spirit of the Cistercian tradition not so much as it is written but as it has been lived for over six decades by a deeply spiritual man. To those who know of Kurisumala Ashram or who have read the biography of Fr. Francis, it will provide a gateway to an understanding of the interior life of this remarkable monk. In particular, his description of the stages of the experience of prayer will certainly be helpful to many who, like him, are lifelong seekers of the unseen God.

Michael Casey, ocso
Tarrawarra Abbey

PROLOGUE

It is never the intention of the founders of a monastery to establish in the Church a new way of religious life, but rather to revive in its original fervor the ancient tradition of monasticism. Similarly, the teachings of Saint Bernard and of the writings of the first Cistercian generations aimed at being only a living and personal echo to the monastic and patristic traditions.

Cistercian spirituality should therefore not be considered in the light of the modern orders or congregations whose ideal of perfection was determined by the particular aim they pursue for the service of the Church. The monk is essentially a disciple who inserts himself into a tradition. The Cistercian Fathers knew this and consciously made themselves disciples of the monks whose examples and teachings are channels of grace for their heirs. Thus it is the whole monastic tradition which is the family wealth of Cistercian monks.

Moses Bar Kepha, a monastic Father of the tenth century in the Antiochean tradition of Mesopotamia, in a homily given after the service of the clothing of monks, traces back the monastic charism to the origins of the human family, to the Cosmic Covenant:

> Understand, my sons,
> what is the monastic charism (*monachatus*)
> and the doctrine of this way of life,
> and let it be known to all who are here.
> The practice of the monastic charism
> is older than the ordination of the monastic habit.
>
> Indeed with our forefathers there was no habit:
> Enoch, Noah, Melchizedek,

Moses, Joshua, Elijah, Daniel and many others practised
continence, abstinence, righteousness, justice and holiness.
Some of them even kept virginity.

And when Christ the Savior of all appeared,
John the Baptist and the holy apostles and evangelists
and their followers
were endowed with the same holy monastic charism.
And, with it, they lived for God.

Later, in the time of Anthony the Great,
the Lord Himself, with other graces,
also gave the monastic habit as the monk's garment.
And all who were clothed in it while being worthy of it
were called monks, and their dwelling places monasteries,
names conveying the austerity of their way of life.

Following Cassian, Saint Bernard, in his *Apologia* (# 24), relates
the origins of the monastic life to the early Church of Jerusalem:

The Monastic Order was the first order in the Church.
It was out of this that the Church grew . . .
The Apostles were its moderators,
and its members were those whom Paul calls "the saints."
It was their practice to keep nothing as private property,
as it is written,
distribution was made to each as each had need.
There was no scope for childish behavior.
All received only as they had need,
so that nothing was useless, much less novel or exotic.
The text states "as each had need."
This means with respect to clothing, something
to cover nakedness and to keep out the cold.
Do you think that they wore silks and satins
or rode on mules with hundreds of gold pieces?
Do you think that their beds had catskin coverlets,
and multicolored quilts
seeing that distribution was made
only as each had need?

Contemporary interpreters of the Acts of the Apostles share the view of Saint Bernard:

> Which components of the three texts of Acts have been given pride of place in monastic literature? The reference to *cor unum et anima una* must recur with the greatest frequency. What about the other elements of the text? How often are they quoted and how are they interpreted? This calls for further study.
>
> Historically, we have here a core of solid information on the original way of life adopted by the earliest Christian community of Jerusalem. This community organized itself along monastic lines. If monasticism is an integral Christian life, must we not also say conversely that Christian life is basically monastic? The consequence would be that every Christian is a monk, at least at heart. The encounter with Indian monasticism invites us to ponder on the implication of this.[1]

Moreover, if the monastic tradition possesses a deep unity, the institutions and the spiritual teachings of the Fathers have given birth to various trends, according to the emphasis put on one or another aspect of the common ideal. The Fathers of Cîteaux have adopted a definite attitude regarding these various trends. The Cistercian tradition is the fruit of their own vocation as well as of the trends of their time. They have conceived an idea of the monastic life which was both traditional and new, and was to be a norm of life for those who followed them. We will try to discern the spiritual trends which gave to the Cistercian ideal its particular features.

Thus it is in the light of the monastic tradition as a whole, but interpreted according to the ideas of the Fathers of Cîteaux, that we intend to explain and describe the monastic ideal. It is not our intention to make a detailed study of the teachings of the Fathers of the monastic life, but rather to take our inspiration from them, in order to frame a doctrine capable of giving life today to the members of our community, taking into account the "signs

---

1. Lucien Legrand, in *The Sign beyond All Signs*, 64. See Acts 2:42-47; 4:32-35; 5:12-16.

of the time," the change of mentality and the doctrinal progress which have taken place in the Church since the beginnings of the monastic life and since the time of the Cistercian Fathers. It is therefore as men of the twentieth century that we will put ourselves under their guidance.

We should like to show here that the monastic life does not consist simply in the fulfillment of some duties or in the practice of certain observances or in conforming to external exercises prescribed by a Rule or by Constitutions. While these provide a useful framework, our lives are the fruit of an unceasing dialogue between God who calls us and our own freedom, the freedom of the children of God. It is a free answer to an incessant call of God, addressing us exteriorly in the person of our abbot and in the directions of the Holy Rule, and interiorly by the intimate promptings of the Holy Spirit, which constitute the New Law engraved in our hearts. This law sets us free from all external compulsion and from the slavery of the law by conforming us in the very depths of our being to the divine will.

The call to interiority is in fact the main character of the New Covenant, already predicted by Jeremiah:

> This is the Covenant I shall make with the house of Israel. I will put my law within them, and I will write it on their hearts, and I will be their God and they shall be my people. (31:31)

We then live not only by fulfilling duties imposed on us, but under the guidance of the Holy Spirit, as Benedict tells us in the conclusion of his chapter on the Ladder of Humility. (See also Ezek 36:26; Heb 10:16.) Obedience to the law and fulfillment of the observances (Mosaic Covenant) remain, keeping us in one body, the body of Christ; but their fulfillment becomes a matter of the heart. This is why we pray so often: "Create a new heart in me, O God; put a new and a steadfast spirit within me" (see Ps 51:10).

The message of this twofold call, exterior and interior, is the same: to go, like Abraham, from our country and our kindred, that is, to break with all attachments here below so that we may always put first God and the values of His Kingdom revealed in the Gospel.

These values are the following: repentance with humility and meekness of heart, forgiveness and compassion, peace and the secret of joy of the Holy Spirit; in one word, God's own life poured into our hearts, as Jesus disclosed in the Beatitudes, the Sermon on the Mount, and the Last Supper discourses.

May this directory, by recalling the deep meaning of the monastic life, help the members of our community to live this perpetual departure to the promised land of our heart, where we meet our Lord, the promised land which is reached only in the measure in which we never cease to make progress toward it.

PART ONE

MONASTIC TRADITION AND CISTERCIAN LIFE

Chapter 1

THE ROOT VOCATION
OF CHRISTIAN DEDICATED LIFE

1. The Fullness of Christian Life

At the outset the monk can be described as "a Christian leading a religious life according to Christ's call to perfection in the Gospel and according to the early tradition of the Church."

The monk is a religious, that is, a Christian well aware of the demands put on him by Christ's discipleship. In his desire to conform to Him, he has entered a state of life in which everything is arranged so as to promote the growth and the flowering of the life of grace, of the Holy Spirit in us. The aim of the religious life is not different from that of a simple Christian life; the religious is not seeking a perfection higher than that offered to the simple Christian. Every Christian has the duty to seek the perfection of charity. What is proper to the religious is that he has chosen a stable way of life in which everything is directed to the pursuit of this aim only.

The religious is not marked off from the simple faithful as one "consecrated," distinguished from one "nonconsecrated." Every baptized person is consecrated, a member of a holy nation and set apart from the ungodly world, the world of evil, in order to belong entirely to God. But the religious, by his profession, is established in a state of life, officially sanctioned by the Church, in order to allow this baptismal consecration to find its full expression and to be worked out in a privileged manner.

The monastic life is also a religious life, but one framed according to the ancient traditions of the Church. This does not mean that it is an antiquated relic of a bygone age, but that its structure was established between the fourth and the twelfth centuries. It is a religious life conceived by the Church, the Fathers of the Church, under the guidance of the Holy Spirit, and it is from this that it draws its permanent value. Just as the doctrinal writings of the Fathers remain for the Church ever-living springs, so the ascetical teachings of the masters of the spiritual life of the first centuries have created a form of religious life which must remain alive in the Church at all times.

What gives to the life and thought of the Church of the Fathers its proper character, its fullness, its all-embracing synthesis, is the absence of specialization. To the monastic life belongs this character of fullness. It is simply a life in which everything is arranged for the pursuit of perfect discipleship, the full flowering of the life of Christ in us, without any kind of specialization. All the means of which it makes use, according to tradition, are directed to this sole aim: renunciation of marriage and of earthly possessions. Solitude and service, prayer and silence, obedience, fasting, vigils, austerity of life, manual labor, liturgical and private prayer, lead the soul toward unceasing prayer, nearness to Jesus, unbroken communion with Him.

The monk is thus distinguished from the religious belonging to a modern institute by the absence of a "secondary aim." Indeed modern religious institutions are usually organized so as to lead their members at the same time to the perfection of charity and to assume for the Church a particular task: education, health care, preaching, works of charity, and the like. Sometimes, even, the founders have dedicated their institute to a particular devotion, such as the cult of reparation to the Sacred Heart of Jesus, the Immaculate Heart of Mary, the adoration of the Blessed Sacrament, or of the Precious Blood, and the relief of souls in purgatory. Because of this, modern institutes, while keeping the principal means established by the Church's tradition to assist in the pursuit of the common and principal aim—the perfection of charity—have reduced the part given to some of these means; for instance, the withdrawal from the world which favors a spiritual atmosphere, the Liturgy of the Hours and private prayer. They gave their life and adapted it to the needs of the "secondary aim."

2. Monastic Life and Contemplative Life

According to the monastic tradition, the phrases "active life" and "contemplative life" do not refer to distinct states of life, distinguished by different "secondary aims" as would be the active apostolate and works of charity on one side, and on the other side the liturgical celebrations and spiritual exercises, corresponding to different vocations. They mean rather two stages, two complementary aspects of the spiritual life, two facets of the same coin. The "active life" is described as the practice of asceticism and virtues, especially fraternal charity; the "contemplative life" is the life of deep union with God, the moving experience of His intimate presence to which a generous ascetical effort usually leads.

In this way, the monastic life is inseparably active and contemplative. It is active, not in the sense that it is organized for a particular ministry in the Church but as consisting, essentially, in the practice of evangelical virtues and brotherly service, as required by the ordinary circumstances of life. It is contemplative, not in the sense that the monk would have as "particular aim" the celebration of the sacred liturgy or the practice of some spiritual exercises, but as directed exclusively to promote a life of deep union with God in which prayer permeates the whole life and is practically identical with the perfection of theological charity.

This being established, there is room, within the monastery, for more active vocations, inclined to the humble service of the brethren in the common life, and for more contemplative vocations attracted by the sacred liturgy or by simple prayer of the heart. This is beautifully illustrated by Saint Bernard in a description which he calls "the cloistral paradise":

> The monastery is truly a paradise, a region fortified with the rampart of discipline. It is a glorious thing to have men living together in the same house, following the same way of life. How good and pleasant it is when brothers live in unity. You will see one of them weeping for his sins, another rejoicing in the praise of God, another tending the needs of all, and another giving instruction to the rest. Here is one who is at

prayer, another is reading. Here is one who is compassionate, and another who inflicts penalties for sins. This is one aflame with love, and that one is valiant in humility. This one remains humble when everything goes well and the other one does not lose his nerve in difficulties. This one works very hard in active tasks, while the other finds quiet in contemplation. (Div. 42:4)

Fourteen styles of monastic living—some of them incompatible, even opposite, observes Fr. Michael Casey. Most communities would recognize their own members in Bernard's list. What is unity? It is that which binds together what is different and unique. Its opposites are envy, competitiveness, petty-mindedness, intolerance, self-justification, self-assertion, and the refusal to be absorbed in community life, which Bernard calls *singularitas*, that is, individualism.

It is left to the spiritual discernment of the superiors to distribute the offices and duties according to this legitimate diversity. It will be advisable, however, to see that brotherly service does not degenerate into activism nor endanger the essentially contemplative orientation of the monastic life. And in case some tasks requiring active service have to be entrusted to souls attracted by a deeper contemplative life, these will have to bear this trial without losing their peace of mind and rather transform all activity into prayer by the deep orientation of their heart to God alone.

3. The Various Forms of Monastic Life

A secluded life is the distinctive mark of the monk in contrast to the first ascetics who lived in the midst of the Christian community during the first three centuries. It was toward the end of the third century, when the ascetics began to withdraw into the desert or to the mountains, that monasticism first asserted itself as a new way of life in the Church. However, as the life of seclusion was led individually, the new institutions soon developed in two ways: the way of the hermit (the recluse or the pilgrim monk) and the way of the cenobites (those who lived in a community).

As such, the cenobitic life is directed rather to the perfection of the "active life" and the eremitical life to be a full flowering of the "contemplative life." It is for this reason that a whole school of monastic spirituality considered the first to be a simple preparation for the second, to which every monk having a real contemplative ideal should aspire.

Origen pleads for, and practiced, contemplation in the world:

> You who follow Christ and imitate Him, You who live in God's word and practise his commandments: you are always in the sanctuary and never leave it. It is not in a place that the sanctuary is to be sought, but in your actions, in your life, in your behavior. If your life is pleasing to God and fulfills his precepts, it matters little whether you are at home or at the market place. It even matters not that you are in the theatre: if you are at the service of God, you are in the sanctuary. Do not doubt it. The ultimate end can be summed up in this way: with a pure heart, become like God in order to draw more and more near to him and to live in him.

Further, because of the dangers threatening the solitary life, many masters of the spiritual life would keep the great majority of monks in the cenobium during their whole lifetime. But at the same time they would enforce seclusion from the world, silence and authentic contemplative life. In addition to that, obedience and the loving submission to his superiors and to his brothers, shown in the details of everyday life, was a path of renunciation which conformed the cenobitic monk intimately to the Christ of the Gospel, meek and humble of heart. Thus community living was the equivalent of the hermit's rigorous solitude. This last view, which spread very early in the West through Cassian, was adopted by the first Cistercians.

Saint Benedict's Rule reflects this view in the first chapter:

> The first kind of monks is that of the cenobites, those who live in monasteries (community) and serve under a Rule and an Abbot. The second kind is that of the anchorites or hermits, those who . . . after their formation in a monastery, having

> learned among many brethren how to fight against the devil, go out well-armed from the ranks of the community to the solitary combat of the desert. . . . to fight single-handed against the vices of the flesh and their own evil thoughts. (RB 1:2-5)

It would not be fair to argue from the social character of Christianity and give cenobitism an exclusive preference, as Saint Basil did. Truly, the cenobium is a distinguished manifestation of the unity of the Mystical Body. But it is a manifestation only, on the level of things that can be seen. The deep reality of the union of all members of Christ in charity transcends all particular realizations, ever imperfect here below and until the Parousia comes; it is given in its all-embracing fullness only in the innermost heart. Therefore, a hermit who possesses a higher degree of charity, who has reached the stage of unceasing prayer, is more deeply united with all people than a cenobite possessing charity in a lesser degree.

The cenobite must therefore be convinced that his relative solitude, which is ensured mainly by silence with respect to his brothers themselves, should help him to enter more deeply into the mystery of the communion of the saints than fraternal exchanges sought indiscriminately. An authentic cenobitic life is expected to favor a personal search for God, a drawing near to the Lord, as we profess on the day of our solemn clothing as a monk, a life with Jesus and in Him. "Abide in Me as I abide in you," said Jesus to His disciples. "I wish to draw near to God. Be good to me, Lord, my trust, that I may recount all Your wonders," proclaims the candidate at the beginning of the sacramental initiation of his clothing as a monk.

4. Models of the Monastic Life

Rather than make use of abstract notions to describe their ideal of life, monks of old used similes or comparisons, as Jesus revealed the mysteries of the Kingdom of God in parables. These soon became traditional as they contained a whole theology of the monastic life.

4.1. The Angelic Life

Christian antiquity described monasticism as the "Angelic Life" because it is organized so as to promote in every possible way detachment from the present world and dedication to the world to come, to the city of the angels and of the saints. The monk's life of divine praise, chastity, poverty, simplicity and single-mindedness is, at the same time, his sign of the preference he gives to the "eschatological" realities, eternal life and the fruit of the new life poured out into his heart by the Holy Spirit. Liturgical prayer as well as silent contemplation are a participation in the liturgy of the heavenly city:

> I think that because of the perfect renunciation of the world which it demands and the singularly lofty spiritual life which it favors and by which it is raised above all other ways of life, [the monastic way] makes those who profess it and love it different from men and similar to angels. It reconstitutes the image of God in man, it configures us to Christ as baptism does. (Saint Bernard, *On Precept and Dispensation*, 54)
>
> The life you profess is a lofty one. It surpasses the heavens, it is on a par with the angels, it is like them in its purity. For you have made a vow not only of holiness, but of the perfection and the completion of holiness. You do not stop at the common precepts, you do not ask only what God commands, but what he wants, investigating the will of God—all that is good, all that is acceptable to him, all that is perfect. Others have the function of serving God; yours is to adhere to him. Others are expected to believe in God, to know him, to love him, to revere him; you are expected to savor him, to understand him, to make his acquaintance, to enjoy him. (William of Saint Thierry, *The Golden Epistle*, 15–16)

Our *Prayer with the Harp of the Spirit* refers repeatedly to our association with the angels, as described in Revelation 8:1-4.[1]

> When the Lamb broke the seventh seal, there was silence in heaven for about half an hour. And I saw the seven angels who

---

1. See also *The Clothing of Monks in the Antiochean Tradition*, 124.

stand before God. They were given seven trumpets. Another angel with a golden censer came and stood at the altar. He was given a great quantity of incense to offer with the prayer of all the saints on the golden altar in front of the throne. And from the angel's hand the smoke of incense went up before God with the prayers of His people. (Rev 8:1-4)

4.2. The Prophetic Life

The monastery is a prophetic place: an anticipation of the world to come, a permanent declaration of a universe remade in God, a universe whose poles are charity and the praise of God, fixed points to which all others are referred. Established in a state of life which anticipates the eschatological destiny of humankind, the monk, thanks to the power of the spirit living in him, witnesses to a prophetic way of life. The Fathers were inclined to see in the prophets of the Old Testament, and especially in Elijah, Elisha and John the Baptist, models and prefigurations of their way of life:

> What shall we say of prophecy? . . . Until John came, there were the Law and the Prophets. Thus says Truth Himself. Yet he who, after Saint John, said, "We know in part and we prophesy in part," was not an adversary but a disciple of truth. Prophecy has ceased, because now we have knowledge, and yet it has not ceased altogether, since we prophesy in part. "When that which is perfect has come, that which is imperfect will be done away with." The prophets prior to John foretold the two comings of the Lord, and nevertheless the two parts of our salvation were not yet entirely known: they remained hidden in the prophecy. Now your way of prophesying, the kind of prophecy to which you have dedicated your lives, is of a high order, as I see it. According to the Apostle's teaching, it consists in regarding not the visible things but the invisible. That is what it really means to prophesy: to walk according to the Spirit, to live by faith, to seek only the goods of heaven instead of those of earth, to forget the past and apply ourselves exclusively to that which is before us. Yes, that is to prophesy in great part. For how can our life be in heaven, if not by the spirit of prophecy? It is thus that the prophets of other times, bridging time by a flight of

thought, launched into the future, separated themselves from their contemporaries and thrilled with joy at the idea of seeing the day of the Lord. They saw it, and this vision inebriated them with joy. The manner of prophesying, . . . demands a superior way of life; for in it one becomes attached to spiritual and eternal realities. (Saint Bernard, *De Diversis*, 37:6-7)

Your state is not some innovation. It is the fruit of the ancient religion, of the perfect piety which is founded in Christ. It is the ancient heritage of the Church of God, foreshown at the time of the prophets and, when the Sun of the new grace was rising, restored and reborn in Saint John the Baptist. (William, *The Golden Epistle*, 11)

4.3. The Apostolic Life (The Life of the Early Church of Jerusalem)

Under the guidance of the Spirit of Pentecost and under the guidance of the apostles who had led a similar common life with Jesus during the years of his messianic ministry, the Christians of the early Church of Jerusalem endeavored to put fully into practice the Lord's teachings on renunciation of earthly goods for the sake of the Kingdom of God, and on giving away one's possessions to the poor. The common life described in the Acts of the Apostles was taken as a sign of the coming of the eschatological times and as the first fruits of the gathering of all the children of God in the heavenly city. To adduce adequate grounds for their way of life, the monks of old liked to turn to this "apostolic life," which they sought to perpetuate in the Church. Even the hermits who distributed their possessions to follow Christ appealed to it. (See Acts 2:42-46; 4:32-35.)

Saint Bernard saw in the life of the early Church of Jerusalem the origin of the monastic order:

The monastic order was the first order of the Church. It was out of this that the Church grew . . . The apostles were her wonderworkers, and her members were those whom Paul calls "the saints." It was their practice to keep nothing as private property, as it is written: Distribution was made to each as each one had need. There was no place for childish behavior. All received only as they had need, so that nothing was useless, and much less novel or unusual. The text says: "As each had need." This means with respect to clothing something to cover nakedness and to keep out the cold. (*Apologia*, 24)

Together with this policy of holding everything in common while sharing according to the needs of each one, there was a deep concern with poverty. In their early documents the Cistercians described themselves as "poor with Christ the poor" and even found fault with any display of splendor in church buildings or in the common way of life:

> O vanity of vanities, a vanity as insane as it is vain! The Church is resplendent in her walls, but in her poor she languishes. She has covered her stones with gold, but has left her children naked. (*Apologia*, 28)

4.4. *The Monk and the Martyr*

For the Christians of the first three centuries, martyrdom was the highest perfection that could be reached by a disciple of Christ who wished to follow his Master to the end. The martyr, or witness, is one who gives the greatest witnessing to Christ by offering his life for the Lord's sake, a man of the Spirit; he enjoys the experience of the power of the risen Christ who triumphs in him over Satan and the world by giving him a love for God stronger than all enticements of the world here below.

When the persecutions came to an end, the monks made an appearance as the successors of the martyrs. They were united with Christ's passion, seeing their monastic life as a war against Satan and a work of love. Martyrdom was considered a second baptism, or a baptism of blood in case the martyr had not yet been baptized, because in it is fully realized the configuration to the death and resurrection of Christ, sacramentally inaugurated at baptism. So, too, the monastic life as a whole was considered a second baptism or the highest fulfillment of baptism as the monk freely unfolded in his life the sacramental mysteries. Later this view was applied to the celebration of the monastic profession.

As a model of the monk in his spiritual combat, the martyr is a model also on account of his contemplation, as contemplation is but the experience of the love of Christ poured out into our hearts by the Holy Spirit. (See the martyrdom of Saint Stephen, especially in Acts 7:54-60.)

Saint John Cassian sums up beautifully the teaching on martyrdom as part of the monastic charism:

> The patience and strictness with which monks remain so devotedly in their profession, once they have taken it up, never fulfilling their own desires, crucifies them daily to this world and makes living martyrs of them. (*Conferences*, 18:7)

5. The Monk in the Church

From what has been said up to now, it appears that in the monastic order the Church reconnects with her origins, not by an archeological return to the past, but by a movement toward that which belongs to her deeper life. She becomes again the Church of the apostles, of the martyrs, of the Fathers. At the same time she reveals more clearly than anywhere else her eschatological character.

In the Church the monastic life is not a ministry or a particular function. Unlike priestly life and married life, it is not based on a particular sacrament. If we consider what belongs to it as proper, it is not to be ranked among the sacramental signs but among the realities of the life of grace signified by the sacraments. The monastic life or, better, the monastery, is the place where everything is organized so that the means of sanctification entrusted by Christ to the Church as a sacred deposit may bear all their fruits in the life of the Spirit.

Therefore monkhood can very truly be said to be at the heart of the Church, summing up, so to say, the whole mystery. The monastic institute stands for the way of life which the Church, as teacher of perfection, offers to him who wishes to live exclusively, and of his own free will, for the full growth of the seeds of grace sown in his heart at baptism and later by the proclamation of the Word of God and the celebration of the Divine

Mysteries. As such, monkhood stands as the most interior aspect of the Church's tradition and it offers a model to all believing Christians.

On the other hand, in the measure in which these means of sanctification bear fruit in him, thanks to his prayer and to the holiness of his life, the monk possesses—as does every friend of God—a distinctive power of intercession which can be regarded as a spiritual priesthood. At the same time the holy monk and the monastery where he lives, by the radiance of spiritual beauty, enjoy a power of attraction on believers who are meeting with trials, but also on those who seek a spiritual renewal by entering more deeply into the mystery of the Kingdom of God and its hidden presence here below, on earth:

> Rid yourselves of all malice and deceit, insincerity and jealousy and recrimination of all kinds. Like newborn infants that you are, you must crave for pure milk—spiritual milk I mean—so that you may grow into salvation, if indeed you have tasted that the Lord is good. Draw near to Him, our Living Stone. Though rejected by mortal ones, He is the Chosen One of God, precious in his sight. Come and let yourselves be built into a spiritual house. Become a holy priesthood, to offer spiritual sacrifices acceptable to God through Jesus Christ. (1 Pet 2:1-4)

Chapter 2

BENEDICTINE MONASTICISM

1. The Monopoly of the Benedictine Rule in the West

The monopoly given to one Rule, that of Saint Benedict, is a thing which is proper to Western monasticism. It also happened later than what is generally believed. It is only gradually, in the course of the seventh and eighth centuries, that the Rule of Saint Benedict asserted itself, at the time of Emperor Charlemagne (800 CE). It was by his power that it was enforced on the majority of the Western monasteries. This adoption occurred even later in some countries like Italy, Spain and Ireland, where the decline of culture and the decadence of institutions had been less serious.

Before that, Western monasticism was in a condition very similar to that of Eastern monasteries today. The life of the monks was framed by a body of ascetical rules, traditional observances and disciplinary regulations enacted by ecclesiastical or civil authorities, to which were usually added local customs. Sometimes, bishops, abbots or assemblies of abbots had codified what appeared to them as essential elements of the monastic tradition and had laid down rules for a particular monastery or group of monasteries. But these rules were never regarded as having a universal value. Often the observances of a particular monastery would be inspired simultaneously by several rules, the system of the *Regula mixta*.

2. Saint Benedict and the Monastic Tradition

For a long time historians believed that the work of Saint Benedict was eminently original and that it was marked off by his will to react against the excessive austerity and insufficient organization

15

which stood in opposition to his Roman mentality of order and discretion, understood as reserve and discernment. At present a better knowledge of ancient monasticism and a genuine sense of history prompt us to appreciate the deeply traditional character of the Benedictine Rule. It is now admitted that Benedict freely used previous monastic rules, particularly the Rule of the Master, which he corrected by leaving out lengthy portions and giving to what he preserved his touch of discretion or discernment, highly praised by Gregory the Great. Benedict codified the tradition of the preceding centuries. By doing this that he proved himself to be a master. It is in this discernment that his originality consists.

The first quality of the Benedictine Rule is that it offers a complete exposition for the good functioning of a monastic community:

Ideal: a school of the Lord's service;

Regulating authority: abbot and council;

Spirituality: centered on humility and obedience in imitation of Christ;

Major occupation: the Opus Dei, the prayer of the Church;

Administration: through prior, cellarer and deans;

Growth of the community: by the formation of new candidates;

Community spirit: mutual obedience, bearing one another's weaknesses, the pure love of brothers, sincere and humble love of the Abbot while having reverence for God.

The second major quality is that the Rule is marked overall by a sense of discretion-discernment, that is, consideration. By this it is related to Pachomius and Basil. No more the ascetic performances of the Desert Fathers, but rather the detachment of a heart in full surrender to the Lord and in readiness for all tasks entrusted to it.

The third quality is that the Rule is balanced. It leads the monk along a royal way by which he is drawing near to God. The abbot's authority is great, but he is given repeated warnings against using it irresponsibly. He has to arrange everything with consideration and discernment—the mother of all virtues—so that "the strong have something to yearn for, and the weak nothing to run from" (RB 64:19). Above all, prayer, work and *lectio divina* are wisely balanced.

In conformity with the literary genre of the ancient monastic rules, the Rule of Saint Benedict is directly concerned only with the first phase of the spiritual life, the "active life," which is to be pursued in a community. It stresses the spirit of humility, obedience and charity which should permeate fraternal relations. But Saint Benedict makes it clear that the monk who faithfully perseveres in the practice of his Rule will one day attain the loftier heights of the contemplative life. And he refers him to Saint John Cassian, whose *Conferences* give detailed teaching on the higher states of the life of prayer attained by the Desert Fathers of Egypt.

3. The Benedictine Tradition

The Rule of Saint Benedict was not propagated by his direct disciples. It was generally adopted as an instrument for reformation in the countries where an indigenous monasticism was already established. It is for this reason that the observance of the Rule had to be adapted to local traditions.

Monachism at the time of Charlemagne (800 CE) and during the two centuries that followed was the fruit of the meeting of the Benedictine text with the Gallican and Anglo-Saxon monastic traditions.

As a whole, Benedictine monachism of the early Middle Ages takes its main character from the growth of the liturgy which reaches its climax at Cluny; but also from a certain toning down of poverty, of simplicity of life and of the spirit of seclusion of the first monks. It developed, nevertheless, a current of real contemplative prayer which had its influence on the renewal of the following age.

Indeed, in the course of the eleventh and twelfth centuries, a vast movement of reformation gathers momentum, aiming at the restoration to a place of honor of solitude, poverty, austerity of life, for the benefit of contemplative interiority: in Italy, Camaldoli and Vallombrosa; in France, Cîteaux and the Grande Chartreuse;

and many others. The aspiration which animates this movement is a return to the origins. Many features, added to the monastic life during the preceding centuries, were maintained and even sometimes hardened: clericalization of the monastic life, strict observance of the Benedictine Rule, uniformity of observances, among others. On the other hand, the way of understanding poverty, the blending by some monks of the eremitical life with itinerant preaching, bear the marks of the time and herald the Franciscan movement.

During the modern age, the various orders and congregations who lay claim to the Rule of Saint Benedict will keep the features acquired by Western monasticism between the seventh and the twelfth centuries. However, besides this they will generally be marked more or less happily by the legislation, the observances and the spirituality of the modern institutes, especially the Jesuits.

Chapter 3

CÎTEAUX

1. The Spirit of Early Cîteaux

Among the monastic reforms of the eleventh and twelfth centuries, Cîteaux is that which enjoyed the greatest expansion and had the deepest influence on the life of the Church. The distinctive features impressed on the Order by the founders and by the spiritual teachers of the second generation (Saint Bernard, Aelred of Rievaulx, William of Saint Thierry, Guerric of Igny, and others) are eminently representative of the contemporary trends of monastic reform. It is good to single out the following characteristics:

1.1. The Concern for Authenticity

The concern for authenticity manifested itself at Cîteaux in the desire to revert to the observance of the Rule in all its purity. Their observance is described as *rectitudo regulae*, which means the straight path of the Rule. Yet it was not an observance of the "letter that kills but of the Spirit that gives life" (2 Cor 3:6), but one inspired by reverence for the Rule, inasmuch as, many centuries after its composition, it remained a carrier of the spirit, as observed very early by Gregory the Great's phrase *discretione praecipua*, "remarkable by its discernment." Discernment is a gift of the Holy Spirit. As Saint Benedict recommended in chapter 73, the early Cistercians took care to reinsert the Rule in the setting of early monastic tradition.

This concern for authenticity was shown also in the liturgy: simple offices as in the Rule, and in the matter of chant, a search for the best *Antiphonarium*. A similar zeal for authenticity appears in Saint Stephen's personal work to establish a better text of the Bible. His own version was considered to be the best for several centuries.

1.2. The Symbiosis between Contemplation and Common Life

Symbiosis means permanent union between organisms (here contemplation and common life), each of which depends for its existence on the other. It is to favor such a symbiosis that, like all the monastic reformers of the time, the founders of Cîteaux wished to settle down in the desert, away from the world. But this eremitic tendency did not exclude the common life. On the contrary, the first Cistercians were deeply attached to brotherly life. They were known as "lovers of the place and of the brothers." However, the seclusion from the world was very strict for the community, and silence was reverently observed so that each one could enjoy solitude in his heart.

Further, this concern for expressing outwardly the bonds of charity and the spiritual communion uniting all the members of the Cistercian family inspired not only the cenobitic status of the monasteries but also the gathering of the various houses in one Order, observing similar customs. The prescriptions of the *Charter of Charity*—the Constitution of the Order—did not originate only from a concern for a common observance in all monasteries, or for erecting a wall of protection against interferences from outside, but above all for providing a visible expression of the union of the souls, unanimity.

1.3. Zeal for Simplicity and Poverty

This is also a common feature of the various monastic reforms of that time. At Cîteaux it expressed itself in the simplicity of the clothing made of undyed wool, simplicity in buildings, simplicity of the sacred vessels, and in the renunciation of ecclesiastical revenues and possessions.

1.4. Austerity of Life

Cîteaux did not follow some of the contemporary eremitical movements in their enthusiasm for afflictive penances, such as self-flagellation or the use of chains or iron belts. But the traditional bodily exercises were faithfully practiced: vigils, fasts and abstinence, and especially manual labor.

1.5. Contemplative Interiority

The spiritual doctrine of the Cistercians of the twelfth century goes back to the most contemplative trends of ancient monachism: Origen, the Fathers of the Desert, Gregory of Nyssa and Maximus the Confessor, Augustine, John Cassian and especially Gregory the Great, monk himself and great pope. They give a distinctive place of honor to fraternal charity, but the key to the Cistercian ideal remains *redire ad cor*, "return to the heart," the experience of the inner taste, the visitation of the Word, the Bridegroom: "Taste and see that the Lord is good" (Ps 34:9). It is the search for these inner riches and glory which explains the love of the Cistercians for silence and solitude, their zeal for poverty, even their renunciation of the splendors of the liturgy.

There is, in this view, common to the whole eremitical movement of the eleventh and twelfth centuries, no contempt for liturgical worship as such, but an ardent desire for spiritual sobriety, a purpose of setting aside all that which threatens to lead the soul to exteriorization, or to blunt the heart's sensitivity to the promptings of the Holy Spirit.

1.6. Mary in the Spiritual Life

In the Cistercian writings of the twelfth century there is no question yet of a particular devotion to Mary, as became fashionable in the following centuries. The early Cistercians, like other monks, never separated the Mystery of the Virgin Mother of God from the Divine Dispensation, the Economy of Salvation, Christ's work of salvation which provides the very substance of the prayer of the Church. Later schools of spirituality tended to invoke the Virgin Mother of God under a particular title proper to themselves. Franciscans, Dominicans, Carmelites and Cistercians all call Mary their Queen. Instead of addressing her as Mother of God, the most beautiful and elevated name of the humble Virgin of Nazareth, they invoke her as Our Lady of Mount Carmel, as Queen of Cîteaux. In popular pictures the founders of the respective orders receive their habit from her. And this was accompanied with a multiplication of feasts, purely devotional feasts not related to the two great events of the Economy of Salvation of which Mary is at the heart: the Annunciation during which the Word of God becomes flesh in her womb, and her bodily Assumption to heaven in which is anticipated the ultimate destiny of the fallen human family.

With an outstanding fervor the first Cistercians contemplated in the feasts of the Blessed Virgin Mary, Mother of God, the perfect model of the human creature restored in Christ. It was from the power of her intercession, humble yet confident, as exemplified at the wedding of Cana in the Gospel, that they expected the grace that would shape Christ in them, so that they would become conformed to Christ. As Mary formed the Word of God into a human being like us, Jesus of Nazareth, she will obtain for those who seek her intercession the grace to be conformed to Christ.

2. The Reforms of the Order of Cîteaux

As with all religious families, the Cistercian Order has, to some extent, departed in the course of the centuries, from its original ideal.

Decadence came. This was due first to a lowering of the standards of fervor, but also to historical circumstances. The thirteenth century in Europe was marked by the growth and expansion of cities. The wars for power were no more between barons and counts with the use of their knights, but between cities. Later political circumstances, tyrannical interferences of rulers, suppression of monasteries or their destruction at the time of revolutions caused much harm.

There were, however, movements of reform like that of La Trappe in France, at the time of Abbot de Rancé in the seventeenth century. Later, during and after the French Revolution, this tradition was saved by Abbot de Lestrange, who wandered through Europe, England, and also to the United States at the head of two communities, one of monks and one of nuns, making foundations on his way which are still flourishing today, for example, Westmalle in Belgium.

The search for a stricter observance was made in order to recover the spirit of the twelfth century in all its purity, as the first Cistercians themselves aimed at observing the Rule of Saint Benedict in its purity. But this ideal was pursued by men who could not avoid being influenced by the trends of their time, marked as it was by rigorous bodily mortification, even self-flagellation.

Their return to the sources was facilitated by the numerous editions, formerly only in manuscripts, published after the invention of the printing press. Indeed, Abbot de Rancé had a vast knowledge of the early monastic tradition, a knowledge more extensive than that of the early Cistercians. But it remains true that these texts were read in the spirit of the time, which was rigorist. However, the fruits of holiness produced at La Trappe bear, nevertheless, witness to the presence of the Holy Spirit. And if the penance of the Trappists was rigorous, we meet also among them numerous souls radiating peace and inner joy, the fruit of a life of personal prayer.

A similar remark must be made about Dom Augustin de Lestrange and his work undertaken during the French Revolution, after 1799. There also, although the realizations did not always match the intentions, these aimed clearly at restoring the observance of early Cîteaux.

It is to this purpose of recovering the spirit of the early Cistercians and of the early monastic tradition that the Cistercian Order of the Strict Observance wished to remain faithful, rather than to the details of observances enacted by Abbot de Rancé and Dom Augustin de Lestrange. These remain, nevertheless, authentic links, carriers of the Spirit, and of the living tradition which connects us to the origins, and they all have a right to our filial reverence. The present Cistercian Order of the Strict Observance is the fruit of a Reunion Chapter called by Pope Leo XIII in 1892.

3. Tradition and Renewal

Reforms and renewals do not originate necessarily from a reaction against decadence. Adaptations and changes more or less serious in the observances can be required simply by the need to take into account the evolution of minds and the historical circumstances. Cîteaux was born from such a situation, and if the Order wishes to remain faithful to the search for authenticity, which was one of the main concerns of the founders, it must remain open to adaptations. These are sometimes required by fidelity to the spirit of the origins and to its proper tradition, at a deeper level, the level of the spirit. A very remarkable example in this respect is the statute of the General Chapter of 1969 declaring authoritatively that the emphasis on uniformity of observances should give place to unity in diversity. This, it was felt, was required by the expansion of the Order to the four quarters of the earth, which began soon after the Second World War, and continued throughout the second half of the twentieth century. This trend was confirmed by the Constitutions of 1990, which in Cst 70 explicitly recommend inculturation:

> Wherever new monasteries are established the founders have to become lovers of that place. Monastic life is not to be bound to any particular form of culture, nor to any political, economic or social system but, as far as possible, what is rightly valued in the local culture should be welcomed, as new means of expressing and enriching the treasure of the Cistercian patrimony.

However, if a tradition is a living reality which has to develop, it must at the same time remain in continuity with the past. The concern for adaptation should never degenerate into an incessant questioning of the structures. The life of deep union with God does not profit from the anxieties and fermentation of the mind caused by often-repeated changes in the observances. Sometimes it will be preferable to uphold some customs which have lost their original purpose. These archaisms, provided they are not too pervasive, are a legitimate and beneficial manifestation of the continuity of tradition. They can be a valuable opportunity to renounce one's self-will and to fashion oneself into the spirit of a true disciple. On the other hand, as the Order has no pastoral ministry, it is less affected than other institutes by the changes in the environment and of mentalities.

Ultimately, if we consider the monastic tradition as a whole, and the particular place held in it by the Cistercians, we will easily detect some permanent features which will have to be preserved in the process of adaptation, whatever the concrete form in which they are expressed. It is indeed generally at times of crisis, and during the reforms that crisis brings about, that the permanent characteristics reveal themselves most regularly. These permanent characteristics of the Cistercian Order can be summed up as the following:

1. Fidelity to the Rule of Saint Benedict and to the ancient monastic tradition;

2. Concern for authenticity in all matters;

3. Love of solitude and silence;

4. Attachment to poverty and simplicity, even in the liturgy;

5. Zeal for sacred reading nourished on the Bible and all the traditional sources;

6. A preference for humble and toilsome manual tasks and for an austere and arduous life;

7. A love for common life with its more compelling duties as well as with the supernatural charm which is proper to it;

8. Love also for the whole Order and its institutions and rules, in the spiritual union of hearts and a certain uniformity of observances;

9. Finally, a fervent veneration of the Blessed Virgin Mary, Mother of God, whom the Order early claimed as its patroness and as Queen of Cîteaux.

4. Conclusion

The Golden Age of Cîteaux was undoubtedly the twelfth century. It is well known that the Cistercians were the pioneering agriculturists of Europe and, in their concern for simplicity, they created an architecture that is still the object of great admiration today. Twelfth-century Cistercian monasteries, well preserved or in ruins, have become part of the State Archeological Departments in France, Italy, the British Isles, Spain and Portugal, as well as in the German-speaking countries and Central Europe.

Their influence on the Church of their time is far more important than what concerns agriculture or architecture. At a time when Cluny suffered a marked decline, Cîteaux became for the Church, the hierarchy and the faithful, a school of sanctity. Further, Cistercian monks and abbots, such as Saint Bernard, showed the way, became the supporters and the animators of the Church's movement of Reform, begun by the popes of the previous century. During the twelfth century, more than one hundred Cistercians were made bishops. These monk-bishops were each given five companions in order to continue to live a community life. They were enrolled also in order to combat heresies. Like Bernard, they preached the holy crusade, whose noble aim was to reconquer the Church of the Resurrection at Jerusalem. This ultimately proved to be a failure, not only because at the end Jerusalem remained in the hands of the Muslims and the Church of the Resurrection their property, but also because on their way to and from the holy land the crusaders looted and pillaged many Orthodox cities, even monasteries on Mount Athos. The sack of Constantinople in 1204 was the most infamous. However, in the twelfth century the Cistercian influence was felt in all spheres of the life of the Church. This century can truly be called the Cistercian century. In the following century the leadership will fall into the hands of the friars: Franciscans and Dominicans; and in the sixteenth century, the time of the Reformation, into the hands of the Jesuits.

The twentieth century witnessed in all the great Orders a reform tending to recover their own particular charism. Such a reform was authoritatively sanctioned by the Second Vatican Council in its Decree on the Appropriate Renewal of Religious

Life. However, it suffered considerably on account of the impact of the global movement of secularization.

5. A View of Benedictine History

The statement in RB 73:5 that indicates Benedict's acceptance of both the ascetical tradition of the desert (Cassian) and the more ecclesial orientation of cenobitism (Basil) is a pointer to a certain polarity within RB. There is evidence of the presence of two opposed ideals or systems of values: *ascetical values*, with the emphasis on renunciation and solitude for unceasing prayer, and what might be called *affirming values*, with the stress on personal growth and community. Ideally, the opposites are held in creative tension by the application of the principles of discernment, moderation and the golden mean, equally removed from two opposite extremes.

The different expressions of the Benedictine charism are due to different combinations of the two diverging principles. Each community has to find its own balance between solitude and community. No single observance can be used as a gauge of fidelity to the Rule. The integrity of the Rule admits of different expressions, as communities respond to local variations.

However, when this pluralism becomes a cloak for lack of effort, decline sets in. Moderation becomes mediocrity, solitude leads to individualism, and community is reduced to living under the same roof. It is then time for a reform. It becomes necessary to reassert the real values, to restore certain neglected observances in order to make the institution a more suitable means of achieving the purpose for which it exists.

Additional Note

In a letter of January 26, 1998, commemorating the ninth centenary of the foundation of Cîteaux, Dom Bernardo Olivera, abbot General wrote the following:

> The primitive documents from Cîteaux, quite apart from any problems they may present to historians, clearly present us with the following ideals:

Authenticity in monastic observance, in the spiritual life and in liturgical life.

Simplicity and poverty in everything, so as to follow, and be poor with, the poor Christ.

Solitude so as to be able to live for God while building up a communion of brothers.

Austerity of life and of work, so as to promote the growth of the New Man.

Conformity to the Rule of Saint Benedict, a conformity that is absolute, that is without additions contrary to the Rule's spirit and letter.

There is no mention in the primitive documents of a literal observance of the Rule. It is a question of keeping it in all its basic demands and of following it in its purity and probity. The probity and purity of the Rule is what constitutes its essence as a practical monastic way to live the Gospel.

PART TWO

THE SCHOOL OF THE LORD'S SERVICE LEADING
TO PERFECT LOVE

Chapter 4

THE GREAT RENUNCIATION

1. Compunction of Heart, Conversion, Renunciation

Tradition gives the name "conversion" to one's entrance into the monastic life. In the New Testament, conversion is the first demand made on people by the announcement of the Good News of salvation: "Be converted, for the kingdom of heaven is at hand." In both cases it is a question of the same thing.

Conversion consists in the complete return to the meaning and direction originally given by God to our life. "Carnal" persons look to the good things of this world for the satisfaction of their innate desire of happiness. But the Gospel brings the announcement that the figure of this world passes: "Even now the axe is laid to the root of the trees." All human activity and all human life which have meaning only with reference to the present world will perish with it. On the other hand, the same Gospel announces to us that, in Christ, the goods of the Kingdom, the divine life communicated to us, are brought within our reach.

Compunction of heart. Thus we come to conceive in our heart a profound sorrow about our having allowed ourselves to wander so far away from God. This compunction of heart will be one of the essential components of the interior attitude of the monk. It is not a question of a detailed recalling of the sins one has committed, nor of a simple emotional reaction of the sensibility in their regard; still less is it a question of a guilt-complex, irrational and oppressive.

Compunction is the first movement that grace causes to spring up from the depths of our heart when, under the impact of the divine intervention in our life, the shell of the heart's insensibility is broken, so that the old "heart of stone" becomes a "heart of flesh."

So this consciousness of the weight of our sin is accompanied by the intimate conviction of the pardon of the Lord who is near to those that are contrite in heart, and who accepts their sacrifice. Thus compunction marks the life of the monk with seriousness and gravity, but also with peace and a hidden joy.

The preference given to the Kingdom of God above attractions of the present world, and the radical independence in regard to created things which it brings, and which is expressed in the act of conversion, strictly demand only the renunciation of sin and its proximate occasions, but it is in the logic of conversion to go much further, if the Lord calls for it. When one has discovered a possession of incomparable value, which alone truly merits the attention of one's heart, it is logical effectively to renounce all the rest, including the most legitimate possessions, because these have, as it were, lost their interest in the presence of this greatest love.

Such is the profound significance of the renunciations which form the object of the evangelical counsels. These are gestures which proclaim the absolute transcendence of the Kingdom of God and the victorious power of the love of Christ. At the same time, they render progress in this love easier. Not that they preserve us from all temptations: on the contrary, in the closed area of the desert, the monk will often have to act against his thoughts, against the suggestions of Satan—a fight more arduous than all others. But effective renunciation frees us from the numerous cares and preoccupations which divert us and prevent us from being attentive to the diverse interior movements which claim our heart.

The great evangelical renunciations which define the religious state have been reduced to three by the tradition of the Church: poverty, chastity, and obedience. The Rule of Saint Benedict does not contradict this, though the enumeration it gives is slightly different: stability, fidelity to the monastic way of life and obedience. Fidelity to the monastic life embraces the totality of the traditional renunciations and observances which make of the monastic life a state of perfection: poverty, chastity, but also solitude, bodily ascesis, the life of silence and of prayer and the rest.

2. Dedicated Chastity

The monk, in binding himself to practice the evangelical counsel of chastity, renounces marriage, and obliges himself to observe the virtue of chastity proper to celibacy.

This renunciation, the most fundamental in many ways, is not motivated by a lack of esteem for bodily realities or by an unwholesome repugnance in their regard, nor by some incapacity of the heart to open itself to a legitimate human love. On the contrary, such renunciation can have value before God and be psychologically sound only if it proceeds solely from a greater love.

It is with a view to dedicating himself exclusively to the love of the Lord, with an undivided heart, that the monk renounces marriage and physical paternity. If his love for the Lord and his faith in the Lord's love for us, which is the root of our own love, begin to grow lukewarm, the chastity of the monk is in danger, or it may only lead to a narrowing and drying up of the heart.

Appreciating this aspect of dedicated celibacy helps us to understand better in what sense chastity is spoken of as an "angelic way of life." It is not at all a question of refusing the monk's bodily condition, but only of recognizing that the present aspect of this condition, involving sexuality and the other biological necessities, do not correspond to God's definitive design for humankind.

In the divine intention, what comes first is the human being glorified both in body and in soul. Our present situation is only provisional, and it renders our earthly probation possible. But it has also the effect of checking our ascent toward God by dividing our heart, and multiplying our needs and desires. This means that we are subject to a variety of physical and emotional servitudes, which prevent us from being fully attentive to God.

This difficulty will disappear entirely only after the resurrection. But those who embrace celibacy and the other ascetical renunciations, by the power of the love of God poured out in their hearts by the Holy Spirit, escape already a part of these servitudes of our present condition. The power of the resurrection is already at work in their bodies, and it confers on them the first fruits of the spiritual liberty of the world to come.

Finally, celibacy, by which we are dedicated entirely to the love of God, transfigures at the same time our love for our fellow beings. It is characteristic of human affectivity, so far as it is not transformed by grace, that it is exclusive, attaching itself to one single person or to a restricted group. But the fact of reserving our heart to God alone universalizes our love for others, without making it lose any of its tender or delicate qualities.

The monk is called to become a "universal brother," whose heart is ready to offer a welcome to all, precisely because it is freed from the overly earthly condition of our affective relations here below.

Later on we shall have occasion to treat of custody of the heart and austerity of life, which are the chief aids toward the practice of dedicated chastity.

3. Evangelical Poverty

The evangelical counsel of poverty has for its object the effective renunciation of the possession of the goods of this world. But since it is not possible for us to do entirely without these goods, the demands of poverty are less absolute than those of consecrated chastity; its practice assumes different modalities according to different religious institutes, and even according to individuals. It must be regulated by the virtue of prudence, which must play its part in determining the actual modalities of exercise, taking into account the concrete circumstances. Without prudence, the ideal of poverty would belong to the sphere of dreams, bereft of realism, and therefore sterile and dangerous.

The significance of this renunciation is complex. It witnesses first of all to the absolute preference given to the riches of the Kingdom of God above earthly riches. It is because the monk knows that the true riches are not those of our earth, but the "treasure in heaven" that he wishes to live poor.

Next it expresses also the abandoning of ourselves to the fatherly providence of God in all that concerns our livelihood: effective poverty is an efficacious symbol of the interior attitude of the "poor" of the Bible, to whom the Good News of salvation is addressed. The poor, in this sense, are those who are deprived of all human security and of all human prestige, and despised on this account by the rich and powerful of this world. They rely only upon God to come to their help. Freed thus from the haunting preoccupation of the morrow, they can apply themselves wholly to their search after God.

The renunciation of earthly possessions further bears witness to the desire, inspired by love, of following Christ in the destitution of Bethlehem, Egypt and Golgotha.

Finally, it has the value of a sign and of a means toward the practice of the love of one's neighbor. If the disciple of Christ renounces his possessions, the purpose is to give the price to the poor, as He Himself asked to those who came to Him: "There is still one thing lacking. Sell what you own and distribute the money to the poor and you will have treasure in heaven" (Luke 18:23). And Saint Athanasius tells us that this is exactly what the young Anthony did.

Almsgiving is inseparable from evangelical poverty. The simple lifestyle of the monks ought to enable them to distribute in alms the surplus from the fruit of their labor. This does not mean that the monastery should accumulate riches or try to develop its means of production to a maximum so as to be in a position to give alms on a large scale. This is hardly the meaning of what Jesus taught his disciples. But it may well happen that the produce of the normal labor of the monks, or the gifts made to the monastery, exceed the needs of the community: this then must be given in alms.

Also from another point of view, poverty is linked to fraternal charity so far as common possession is a privileged method of signifying communion of souls and of realizing the ideal of the primitive community of Jerusalem.

The practice of evangelical poverty, as applied to cenobites by tradition, can be reduced to the following points, keeping in mind Saint Benedict's teaching: to the question of whether monks ought to have anything of their own, he answers that "this vice of private property especially is to be cut out of the monastery by the roots" (RB 33:1).

First, to possess nothing as one's own, but always in common with one's brothers. This giving up of private possession is not merely a juridical formality to be gone through at the time of the profession: it is a necessity of our daily life. And so a monk should see to it with an extreme delicacy that he does not seek his own comfort by appropriating anything to himself in one way or another, thus causing trouble to the brethren and compromising the meaning of community life. For instance, one ought to make it a rule not to borrow anything, such as books or tools, without informing those in charge, to put those things back in their place and in good condition after use, to take good care of all things as though they were "sacred vessels of the altar," because they belong to the house of God. We ought to love the countless little annoyances which can arise from this common use of material things, because it is most valuable for divesting us of our self-love and for modeling our heart on the heart of Christ.

Second, to use material things in dependence on authority. It belongs to the condition of the poor to depend on another. In the monastic life, to look to the abbot for everything will be a concrete way of exercising a filial and loving self-surrender to the heavenly Father. It is to be expected that this dependence will bring some annoyance and some privations; but it will also lead to a certain hidden joy and an interior liberty which we ought to learn to discover. For the rest, the monk who is seeking God truly can have the certainty, based on faith in the word of our Lord, that he will never be deprived of what is really necessary to him, through the possible incomprehension or incompetence of his superior.

Here again there is need for a great delicacy of soul. This is expressed by our willingness

Not to give or receive anything without the necessary authorization.

To render an exact account of one's expenses.

To avoid by all means having recourse to the generosity of relations or friends and exerting pressure on superiors for obtaining, for personal use, things, even useful, which one could not receive through the normal channels of obedience.

Third, to be satisfied with little and to behave as a man who is detached from earthly goods. The monk ought always to prefer to have less than more, to be happy to have to do without something, to receive all things with thanksgiving, far from claiming anything as one's due. This love of poverty ought to be put into practice equally at the community level, but without stinginess and pettiness. We ought to avoid undue economizing in regard to the quality of the food, lighting and so forth, but also we ought to eliminate from our midst everything that looks like wastage. It is inevitable that a numerous community, which has to live by its labor, possesses buildings, land and machines which could not be had by a poor farmer or artisan. But if the earning of our livelihood will permit it, we should be content with poorer means of production than those which a similar secular enterprise will make use of. We do not look for the prestige which the most modern equipment brings, if we can do without this. While the monk ought not to live as a parasite on society, he is not obliged either to justify his existence by keeping himself in the forefront of technical progress.

Since monastic poverty is essentially the efficacious sign of an interior attitude, it does not necessarily coincide with economy, spending less. An object may be cheap, but by its showy character it may be out of keeping with the spirit of poverty, while sort, another more costly but simpler and plainer, will lead the monk who uses it more securely toward his goal of acquiring the disposition and mentality of the poor. Sometimes it will be necessary to incur the expense of buying something ordinary and of a reasonable price, rather than seek to receive as a gift a luxurious substitute. Finally, it would be exactly the opposite of evangelical poverty to show oneself greedy for gain, to want to sell as dear as possible, to haggle over the price of what one is buying.

Father Michael Casey (in *CSQ* 33:4, p. 427–38) sums up the understanding of poverty in the writings of Saint Bernard as follows:

> 1. Disinterest, detachment from material things. The atmosphere of early Cîteaux, and soon later Clairvaux, suited him, though he suffered serious illness.

2. Voluntary poverty is one of each individual monk's virtues. It should be part of his life.

3. Poverty implies
    (a) the personal disposition of being a servant, as Jesus said: "I came not to be served but to serve."
    (b) On account of this it takes on a painful quality, demanding vigilant and constant struggle; it is part of the spiritual combat.

4. On poverty depends a total union with Jesus. And this helps us to overcome in the struggle, poverty becoming a gift of God.

5. Poverty's ultimate fulfillment is the joy of anticipating the Kingdom of God, in the footsteps of Jesus' words in the Sermon of the Mount: "Blessed are the poor in spirit, for theirs is the Kingdom of God."

4. Humility and Monastic Obedience

Humility is the fundamental attitude of the Christian. Those who tend toward perfection should acquire a deeper and deeper sense of their own utter dependence upon God, and express this by an entire submission to God's will. They ought to be happy to recognize that they cannot glory in anything, or attribute any of their good qualities to themselves. In their relations with others, they ought similarly to renounce all spirit of domination, all desire of imposing their own views on them. Only then can a community of monks arrive at unity, concord, and unanimity, in communion with the divine will.

This renunciation of all pretensions based on pride is required of every monk. The monk goes even further and renounces effectively the right to assert himself and to claim independence even in those domains where a person may do so legitimately. Thus the monastic life is a state of humility, and it is this chiefly through obedience. Saint Benedict is very eloquent on this subject. In one of the last chapters of the Rule, he prescribes mutual obedience:

Obedience is a blessing to be shown by all, not only to the Abbot but also to one another as brothers, since we know that

it is by this way of obedience that we go to God. (RB 71:1. See
also the prologue and chapters 5 and 73.)

By obedience, the monk gives up his own way of looking at
things and his own preferences, even legitimate, in order to submit himself to the will of another.

Monastic obedience is not merely a social virtue, calculated to
promote the common good by the submission of all to the legitimate authority. It also has a pedagogical aspect. Since everything
in the life of the monk is organized in view of the acquisition
of the perfect love of God (RB 7:67), it is normal that, even in
the details of everyday life (food, sleep, work), the disciple submits himself with docility to the prescriptions of an experienced
master, capable of discerning the will of God for him and thus
holding, in regard to him, the place of Christ.

If, however, this were the exclusive purpose of monastic obedience, the monk could free himself from it in proportion as he
approaches a certain spiritual maturity and becomes more apt
to guide himself according to the interior lights received from
the Holy Spirit. Such indeed was the case of the hermits who left
the monastery after a sufficient probation. But there exists for
the monk another motive for renouncing the legitimate exercise
of his autonomy: this renunciation freely made is the efficacious
sign of a perfect interior humility, of a fundamental disposition
of self-effacement and self-forgetfulness, in imitation of our Lord
who humbled Himself and became obedient even unto death.

At the same time, this giving up of free self-determination is
the witness to the absolute preference one gives to the interior
liberty by which one is fully conformed to the divine will in all
things, above all other forms of a simply human liberty.

There is nothing more efficacious than this attitude for drying
up all the passions at their source, namely, self-will. At the same
time, it makes the soul simple, frees it from countless preoccupations, and prepares the way for perfect purity of heart. That
is why the cenobitic tradition has judged it profitable not only
to make of the renunciation of self-will the cornerstone of the
formation of a novice, but also to keep the monk all through

his life in this submission to superiors and even to his brethren: "Let the brothers compete earnestly in obedience to one another" (RB 72:6).

However, monastic obedience has nothing infantile about it. It does not proceed from a lack of character but from the preference given to the love of Christ, the love that impels us to imitate him in his obedience, and to an eminently evangelical value: humility of heart. This is combined with the highest spiritual liberty, since the monk does not bow to an external pressure against his own will but submits himself to another with the ease and spontaneity of love.

Moreover, the perfection of obedience requires that we do not carry it out as a material and mechanical practice. It is normal that the superior should involve the monk with this search after the will of God. Consequently, as long as an order has not been formulated in a definitive and irrevocable manner, it is legitimate, and often better, to expose to the superior, after having reflected and prayed, what we ourselves believe to be preferable. Once the order has been given, whether it agrees with our own views or not, we must apply all our resources of intelligence and initiative to the task of executing the order in the best way possible, in the spirit of perfect submission. Saint Benedict treats this subject with his usual discernment in chapter 68.

It is, above all, when it is a question of asking for permissions and exceptions that the practice of obedience will demand of the monk a personal search for the will of God. The consent of the superior makes the authorization given by him lawful, only if the monk truly believes, before God, that he ought to have asked for it. This sense of responsibility, which ought to be present in all obedience that is truly spiritual, will induce the monk not to want to settle by authority all the cases that might present themselves to him. Where it is a question merely of applying some general directives or a point of rule to a concrete circumstance, we ought to be able to make use of reflection and healthy initiative.

Finally, we ought to be on our guard against reducing all, in the religious observances, to a matter of obedience, and of blind obedience at that. We ought to try to understand, whenever possible, the meaning of what is required of us. Thus, for instance, we are not expected to conform ourselves to the different postures prescribed for liturgical prayer simply because they are prescribed. We should take the trouble to realize how they are the necessary symbol of an interior attitude of reverence toward God and of contemplative attention. Similarly, in regard to other observances, we should apply ourselves to understand and personally to put into practice the intentions of poverty, of fraternal charity, of the keeping of silence, etc. It is these intentions that caused the practices to be adopted by our Fathers in the first place.

5. Solitude and Silence, with Universal Brotherly Love

Effective separation from the world is one of the most characteristic marks of the monastic life. On it, as on poverty, the first Cistercians laid special emphasis in their formulation of their ideals.

A first aspect of this separation from the world is what ancient tradition called "voluntary exile" (*xeniteia, peregrinatio*). Very exceptionally, certain monks have been called by the Holy Spirit to practice this form of ascesis to the letter by renouncing all permanent habitation. Note, however, that pilgrim-monks are not to be confused with "gyrovagues," who are counterfeits and caricatures.

Every monk is also, like Abraham, and the Hebrews in the desert, a pilgrim who has effectively renounced having a home here on earth. His only true fatherland is henceforth the Jerusalem on high, whose mystery is intimated here and now in the depths of his heart where the Lord has taken up His abode.

To be "at home" signifies finding ourselves in safety in a human environment which is connatural to us, to which we are attached by bonds of human affection, a place where we are known and esteemed, and of which we share the mentality, the peculiarities, even the social and racial prejudices. Consequently, we feel ourselves fully at ease there; we are conscious of being able to play our part there, of possessing rights there and of enjoying a natural security.

Now the monk has renounced all this in order to be perpetually in the state of "passage," of Passover, as Jesus instituted it.

We are on the way toward the true Promised Land. The monk must be careful not to create once again in the monastery the former kind of " home" that is simply human. Without prejudice to fraternal charity and a supernatural spirit of community, he must always keep in the monastery something of reserve and the discretion of a stranger, by not seeking to establish with his brethren bonds of intimacy based on purely human affinities and marked by a certain exclusiveness, by not interfering with what does not concern him, by not demanding anything for himself as his right, by using nothing as private property.

Next, separation from the world requires that the monk live in solitude, a seclusion consisting very especially in not getting entangled in secular life and affairs, so that he may be possessed of this exterior calm and peace which lead to tranquility of heart. Various degrees of this separation from the world are possible. Cîteaux wanted a very radical form of it, prescribing that the monasteries should be built away from centers of population, and limiting as much as possible the contacts of the monks with the world. We ought to remain faithful to this.

At the same time we should uphold the sacred tradition of monastic hospitality, receiving all those who seek relief, or are in need of material or spiritual help or come for a renewal of life. And this should be done in such a way that we avoid allowing the fever of worldly life to insinuate itself in the life of the community. And for this a discerning observance of silence should be preserved.

Solitude is the place where God communicates Himself to the soul: that is why the monastic Fathers used to speak of the *paradisus claustralis*, the "paradise of the cloister." But we should not be deceived by such expressions. The desert is also the place of the most arduous spiritual combat. Assuredly, withdrawing into solitude delivers the monk from the temptations which have their source in the contaminated spirit of the world, of our consumerist society, and in the presence of objects which awaken and even stimulate the passions. Still, the monk flees less from the occasions of sin as such than from the state of dissipation, of unconcern or inattention to the divine will and unawareness of the movements of the heart. He flees from what prevents him from living alone with himself in the presence of his heavenly Father, as Saint Gregory wrote of Saint Benedict: he flees from the innumerable enticements which, in the world, draw us unceasingly outside ourselves and distract us from the essential things.

Solitude, on the contrary, permits a man to be attentive to himself. But what he finds at first in the desert is not peace and repose in God, but struggle. Then indeed are revealed, under the form of "thoughts" and evil suggestions, all the unruly tendencies that he had borne within himself without having paid attention. This is a salutary revelation, since it makes the fight possible by drawing us out of a fatal unconsciousness. At the same time, moreover, the soul is made more attentive to the divine precepts and to the interior inspirations of the Holy Spirit which incline it to humility and obedience and enable it to resist the opposite solicitations successfully.

The meaning of solitude is well expressed in the message of monks to the Synod of 1967:

> While the contemplative withdraws from the world, this does not mean that he deserts either it or his fellow-men. He remains wholly rooted in the earth on which he is born, whose riches he has inherited, whose cares and aspirations he has tried to make his own. He withdraws from it in order to place himself more intensely at the divine source from which the forces that drive the world onwards originate, and to understand in this light the great designs of humankind. For it is in the desert that the soul most often receives its deepest inspirations. It was in the desert that God fashioned his people. It was to the desert he brought his people back after their sin, in order to "allure her, and speak to her tenderly" (Hos. 2:14). It was in the desert, too, that the Lord Jesus, after he had overcome the devil, displayed all his power and foreshadowed the victory of His Passover.

If solitude is to bear its fruits, it must be accompanied by the practice of silence, especially when it is lived in common with the brethren. For the cenobite, silence takes the place of the hermitage.

Silence is at first a discipline which the monk must impose on himself. The usages of the Order have rightly determined to which persons the monk may speak, at what times, in what places, and in what manner. But silence should not be merely a rule to be observed on account of exterior pressure. Gradually, it must become a profound need, a demand of the heart. A certain atmosphere of silence is the living milieu outside of which a contemplative soul could hardly find itself at ease.

The man of prayer will not only keep within the limits fixed by the rule, but will also know, as it were by instinct, the measure to observe in the use of words for avoiding all excessive exteriorization, all that could injure the quality of the prayerful atmosphere of the community.

6. Stability

This idea of stability was not a creation of Saint Benedict. The Desert Fathers themselves had often insisted on the necessity for the monk not to change his place easily. In fact, this stability is needed if solitude is to attain its end, which is to achieve the calm and recollection of one's whole being. It is moreover a precious guarantee of perseverance and of continuance in ascetic discipline.

Its most redoubtable enemy is precisely *acedia*, that weariness in face of spiritual effort which often makes us conceive a dislike for the place where we are, and suggests a thousand pretexts for having a change. Faced with such a temptation, the monk ought to force himself with great courage to persevere in his present place, even if it seems to him that he derives no profit from it. This first victory will help him to recover interior serenity little by little.

In the cenobitic life the accent has been put even more strongly on stability: by his profession, the monk contracts with his community a union, of which the Holy Spirit is the bond, and which is a sign of the unity of the Mystical Body, whose full manifestation is reserved for the Parousia.

In virtue of this signification, the bond is indissoluble in itself, as that which binds together the members of a living organism. And so tradition has never hesitated to establish a certain analogy between this entirely spiritual union and that of the spouses in marriage, of which the indissolubility is founded similarly on its value as a sign in regard to the mystery of Christ's union with the Church.

However, the purpose of the cenobitic institution is above all, for each monk, to pursue the full development of the divine life received at baptism; like baptism it is a work of the Holy Spirit. But this work is to be achieved by the cooperation of grace and personal freedom, through the formation received from the community and its spiritual fathers.

This is why stability is not an absolute value. It is subordinated to the conversion of one's way of life and to the true exigencies of the monk's progress in interior charity. It is opposed to all departure from a place motivated by infidelity to the ideal by which the community lives: inconstancy, lack of generosity in putting up with the trials of community life, and the like. But it does not forbid exceptional changes of place, inspired by a higher motive, especially the passage to a stricter way of life, if this is in answer to a call of the Holy Spirit, duly recognized. Other cases may present themselves; to judge them belongs to the conscience of the monk, of his spiritual father and of his superiors.

7. The Monastic Habit: Symbol of Renunciation

Almost from the very beginning of their institution, monks adopted a dress that distinguishes them from seculars and from clerics. By its simplicity and poverty the monk's dress becomes a sign of his life, a life of renunciation. No doubt, the legitimate fixation of certain usages and the evolution of customs have resulted in the monastic habit no longer being as expressive of renunciation as at the beginning. Nevertheless, the monk should rejoice when the occasion is given him to wear in the monastery clothes that are poor and worn out.

Further, the ancient monks loved to attach to the different parts of their dress a particular symbolism related to the essential dispositions which shine in the monastic charism. This appears especially in our Ritual of the Clothing of Monks. There is first a stripping of the former dress, which signifies the casting off of the old nature. There follows a clothing symbolizing the "clothing in the new man." While the belt is put around the monk's waist, the Lord is asked to gird with uprightness, true faith and strength against all the shameful passions. The headgear is related to Christ's crown of thorns, evoking His humiliation. And when he is clothed in the outer garment, the prayer is that the Lord may clothe him in the robe of glory by the power of the Holy Spirit. At Cîteaux it was above all the cowl that received a symbolic value. It was not a choir dress but the monastic habit properly so called. One saw in it, at the same time, an angelic garb, evoking the six wings of the seraphim of Isaiah's vision, and an image of the cross, which the monk wished to carry constantly in his body as well as in his heart.

The wearing of a religious dress is a sign which can help the monk to realize very efficaciously his condition as "one separated," the citizen of a city other than the earthly city. Moreover, since it has been bequeathed to us by our Fathers, it is also a sign through which something of their spirit is communicated to us. Ancient monachism had well understood that the gesture by which the abbot clothed the new monk with the habit on the day of his profession was the symbol of the transmission of a spiritual grace inherited from the Fathers of old.

The spiritual meaning or quality of the monastic clothing goes back to the great prophets Elijah and Elisha. Elijah calls his disciple Elisha—while he was plowing his fields—by throwing his cloak or mantle over him. At the time of his ascent to heaven when he is separated from his disciple, he first performs a miracle with his cloak, separating the waters of the Jordan to cross to the other side. And while ascending he drops his cloak, leaving it as a sign of the gift of his spirit.

Chapter 5

THE MONASTERY,
SCHOOL OF THE LORD'S SERVICE

1. The Spiritual Fatherhood of the Abbot

The renunciations which the monk accepts when he embraces the monastic life are only the point of departure for the combat which he undertakes for the purpose of responding to the grace of his baptism and of becoming a monk not only according to the habit, but more so according to the heart. This occurs by the unification of his whole being in the divinizing charity, as Saint Ephrem prayed:

> Let prayer purify the gloomy thoughts.
> Let faith wipe clean the outward senses,
> and let man, who is one, but suffered to be divided,
> collect himself, Lord, and become one before you. (*On Faith*, 20)

To enter into this combat all by oneself would be to expose oneself to all the illusions of self-will, outside the case of an exceptional call of grace. That is why the first step of the aspirant to the monastic life is to set about looking for a spiritual father who will be able to guide him in discerning the origin of the diverse movements that go on in his soul; one who will teach him to renounce self-will.

The spiritual father played an essential role in ancient monastic spirituality, precisely because the objective is not simply to make sure that the monk observes a certain number of rules and general precepts within the framework of a given life, but to bring him to enter into his own heart more and more, to conduct himself in all things according to his conscience animated by the work of the Holy Spirit. Such an education requires a delicate apprenticeship "in discernment of spirits and a universal renunciation of self-will."

Originally, the authority of the spiritual father was based, above all, on his personal experience of the ways of holiness. He had received the full effusion of the Spirit at the end of a long spiritual combat, to which he himself had been initiated by another spiritual father. Thereafter he could bring forth children to whom he transmitted this Spirit. He did this by his directives, which were characterized—

1. by a spiritual clairvoyance;
2. by his prayer, the efficacy of which was conditioned at once by his own holiness and by the simple faith of the disciples; and
3. by the radiance of his whole life on the simple faith of the disciples.

For his disciples, the spiritual father truly holds the place of Christ. So the grouping of the former round the latter recalls spontaneously the common life of the apostles gathered round the Master during His earthly life—that common life which was prolonged in the life of the primitive Church of Jerusalem. Certain spiritual fathers, particularly aware of the advantages arising from the constant exercise of submission and of fraternal charity for the supernatural education of souls, were thus brought to unite their children in a fraternal community quite strongly organized. Such is the fatherhood of the abbot in regard to each of his monks.

No doubt, the evolution of the primitive grouping of the monks around a charismatic spiritual father into a regular cenobitic monastery destined, as institution, to survive the persons composing it has brought about some modifications of the notion of the spiritual father. The abbot of the cenobitic community must still be a veritable man of God.

However, the abbot no longer holds his authority solely from the Holy Spirit but also from the hierarchical Church, which has received from its Divine Founder the mission of conducting souls to perfection, and which communicates to the abbot the juridical power which associates him with this mission. The role of the bishop in the rite of blessing for a new abbot gives felicitous expression to this insertion of the abbot's function into the ecclesiastical organization.

The abbot also finds himself invested with administrative functions which can become absorbing. It must not be forgotten, however, that these functions are derived directly from the spiritual ministry which belongs to him, and they can be understood properly only in the light of the double significance of obedience mentioned above.

On the one hand, the monk is a disciple who embraces a way of life where everything—including work, food and sleep—is organized in view of his spiritual progress. It is normal, therefore, that the master, to whom he has confided himself, exercises his authority in all these domains. On the other hand, the love of Christ, obedient even unto death, has induced the monk to renounce a legitimate autonomy; on this account also, it is only proper that the abbot takes care of the temporal affairs of the cenobitic community.

This does not mean that the abbot is possessed of unrestricted authority. First of all, he must be guided by the Word of God, and conform himself to the legislation of the Church and of the Order. Moreover, the educative character of his functions requires that he should often involve his monks in the search for the divine will. But the necessity for the abbot thus to involve the monks, individually and collectively, in the decisions that he takes, and to do this with supernatural prudence, is based, much more profoundly, on the very nature of the cenobitic community.

The monastic community is not modeled on the natural monarchical societies, nor even on the Roman *familia*. It is a body animated by the Spirit, where no one may act in a solitary fashion, not even the abbot as the representative of the Head of the Body. Each decision of the abbot must be the expression of an intention of the Spirit in regard to an individual or the community, and consequently it must respond to an intimate motion of this

Spirit in each of those who are concerned in this decision. It is normal that they all cooperate, in their different capacities and ways, with this effort of search.

Nevertheless, the final discernment remains solely within the power of the abbot, outside the case where the formal consent of the community is required by canon law. The consultation of the brethren and the consultation of the elders mentioned by the Rule of Saint Benedict appear thus as the expression of the profound nature of the function exercised by the abbot in the community.

The abbot is at the same time the representative of Christ for his monks, and the organ charged with the authoritative formulation of the divine will, which the Holy Spirit manifests in the heart of each of the members of the community, in view of the union of all.

Hence, the abbot may be said to be the concrete center of the charity of the cenobitic community, the personification of their love for one another. That is why the monk is expected to have for the abbot a humble and sincere love (RB 72), which is to express itself in a docility and an obedience as perfect as possible in regard to him and in regard to his representatives. Union with the abbot is the instrument and the indispensable symbol of the invisible union of the monk with Christ and with the whole Mystical Body. It is the fundamental condition for the sanctification of the monk and for the witness of the community to the Kingdom of God.

2. The Abbot and His Collaborators

Even when he is at the head of a numerous community, the abbot remains truly the spiritual father of his monks. He exercises this fatherhood in a manner which can be very efficacious, by the teaching he gives to the whole community and by all the acts of his government, which ought always to be ordained to the spiritual good of souls. It is for him to give the community a spirit, to create an atmosphere which facilitates the growing of each one into a full spiritual maturity.

It is then extremely desirable that the monks open their conscience to their abbot and manifest their thoughts to him, so that he can fulfill for them a ministry of personal direction. The pressure of his occupations, however, will not always permit him to do this with all the necessary assiduity. Moreover, full openness of conscience requires between the monk and his spiritual father a certain affinity of soul, a spontaneous confidence, the lack of which cannot always be supplied even by a strong spirit of faith, without any culpability on the part of the subject. That is why the cenobitic tradition and the legislation of the Church have allowed that there should be in the monastery other spiritual fathers than the abbot, whom the monk can approach with perfect liberty.

The role of these spiritual fathers, however, can have meaning only with reference to that of the abbot. They are only his prolongation, and, if they truly represent Christ before their children, they receive this function from the abbot, and they exercise it only in strict union with him.

Surely, they keep their own personality, and even the fruitfulness of their ministry is partly conditioned by this, insofar as it renders them better able to understand particular spiritual temperaments. But these legitimate particularities ought never to degenerate into a partisan spirit which would isolate their spiritual children from the abbot and from the community as a whole. Their teaching ought to be in the nature of a prolongation of that of the abbot, and be exercised in conformity with his spirit. Nothing could be more harmful for a monk than to be made aware of a serious conflict among those who have the mission to guide him.

Similar remarks must be made on the subject of the other collaborators whom the abbot associates with himself for the government of the monastery and the management of its temporal affairs: prior, cellarer and other officers. Though their functions have to do with what belongs to the external forum, these different officers should always remember that even the most material realities are themselves, in the monastery, ordained to the good of souls. The exercise of their charge or the management of the office entrusted to them is, therefore, still a form of participation in the spiritual fatherhood of the abbot. Whatever might be the relative autonomy which they enjoy sometimes, they must be careful never to act in some sort on their own responsibility, but always in dependence on the abbot and his spirit.

3. Fraternal Life

The cenobitic monastery is the school of the Lord's service and, as such, it is ordered to the personal sanctification of each of its members. In no way can it be said that here the individual is subordinated to the community or absorbed by it. But Christian perfection is inseparable union with God and union with people in God. Fraternal charity is an integral part of this perfection. It has its final flowering in the communion of saints. The progress in holiness of each of the members of the Mystical Body of Christ concerns all the others at the same time. Each one is enriched by the graces of all.

That is why the community, formed by the monks grouped around the abbot, is, at the same time, the sign and the means of the realization of this invisible communion of which the principle and supreme exemplar is the Holy Trinity. The monastic community constitutes a milieu particularly adapted to the development of deifying charity in the heart of each one.

The daily exercise of fraternal charity, such as is required by the mutual support and the humble service of our brethren, demands a complete renunciation of our self-will, and constitutes the ascetic discipline that is most efficacious for purifying us from our self-centered tendencies. For this reason, it is at the same time the surest way of approach to an authentic contemplation. God is love, and it is only in the measure in which we love our brethren that we can obtain, in the silence of prayer and even in the midst of our occupations, some experience of that which God is.

Still, it is not in devotedness and service that fraternal charity essentially consists, but in a disposition of the heart. Here again, it is a question above all of discovering in the depths of our soul an inclination awakened in us by the Holy Spirit, and of letting it transfigure our whole life little by little, by striving to be always more docile to it. As Saint Benedict says in the conclusion of the chapter on humility: "No longer will [the monk's] motive be the fear of hell, but rather the love of Christ, good habit and delight in the virtues which the Lord will deign to show forth by the Holy Spirit in his servants, now cleansed from vice and sin" (RB 7:69-70).

The first component of this profound attitude which the Spirit inspires in us is humility toward our neighbor. There are few instructions that are repeated so often in the ancient monastic literature as that of condemning oneself and not judging others. Without this foundation, nothing of lasting value can be built up in the spiritual life. There is no authentic conversion without compunction of heart. Only if we have the painful experience of the weight of our own faults, shall we turn away, as by instinct, from all severe estimation of other people.

Pride and self-complacency must necessarily incline us toward harshness in our judgments. On the contrary, humility of heart purifies our view and makes us discover spontaneously all the good in our brothers, which is hidden beneath a covering more or less thick but always superficial. This good is nothing but the radiation of the presence of Christ in them. Thus each of them becomes for us like a burning bush manifesting something of the splendor of God. If God is truly present in our heart, it is impossible that he should not reveal himself to us also in our brothers. If the experience of his sweetness which we believe ourselves to have in the depth of our conscience is authentic, we shall also experience something of this sweetness in our brothers.

To love our brothers in God is, therefore, to love them because we discover in them the traces of the love with which God loves them. So a charity truly supernatural must be universal, like the divine love. An affection which proceeds merely from the sensibility or from self-interest is necessarily exclusive, and often inconstant. The love which springs from a heart purified by grace extends itself to all and shares in the fidelity of God. Supernatural charity surely admits of degrees, an order in affection and intimacy; but this will never be to the detriment of the universality of love.

Love also tends to sharing. To look for some return, and to rejoice in it simply, is more conformable to humility and to that trust in others which ought to suffuse our love.But our charity ought never to limit itself to waiting for the initiative of others, or grow weary of ingratitude. "Like our Lord, we ought to be the first to love and to pardon, and we should extend our love, with a sort of predilection, to the most abandoned, to those from whom we cannot expect any advantage."

Finally, true love of our enemies, of all those from whom we have had to suffer, will be the touchstone of the supernatural quality of our love of neighbor, and therefore of the authenticity of our whole spiritual life.

To discover and to love Christ thus in all our brothers is not to love them in an anonymous and impersonal fashion—for the goodness, the good desires, the supernatural attractiveness that we perceive in them are, at the same time, the work of the Holy Spirit and the profoundest and truest expression of their own personality. That is why one who is humble is full of understanding, and has a kind of gift of revealing to others the best they have in themselves. His sensibility, the human delicacy of his affection, is not dried up, but only purified from all self-seeking.

This humble love should become the soul of all the manifestations of fraternal charity. Thanks to it, acts of mutual consideration will no longer be simple human politeness, but respect and admiration for the presence of God in our brothers. The use of words will no longer be an occasion of speaking ill, but a quiet manifestation of love and of affability toward all.

Fraternal correction—remarks made to the chapter or individually—will not be negative criticism, but an attempt at helping our brethren so that the good that is in them may triumph over what is left of the old man.

In the relationships of the common life, the monk will be ready to yield to the wishes of his brothers rather than to his own, and will be disposed to acknowledge his mistakes, to accept quietly a wound inflicted on self-love, to forgive as God has forgiven him.

The service of the brothers that we have to perform in the community is the fruit of this humble love, and not the expression of a natural liveliness which disguises itself as devotedness and the doing of one's duty of state, but which is in danger of being no more than subtle self-seeking. If our love is humble, this service itself will become an authentic practice of contemplation.

What causes dissipation and prevents us from recollecting ourselves in God is less the multiplicity of our occupations than the absence of interior unity. If our heart is truly oriented toward God, our work will be done without feverishness, without agitation or preoccupation. We shall also be able to establish a hierarchy among our occupations, and sometimes to give up or finish quickly some work which perhaps appealed most to our heart or seemed to us most urgent, but which, in the light of God, appeared to us as really secondary.

We shall be able to create a certain balanced rhythm of the spiritual life and find those indispensable moments of silent prayer. What interferes with prayer is more often not the lack of time but a lack of order in our occupations. The cause is an interior state of tension and agitation which does not help the real efficiency of our work in any way, but which shows that we are seeking ourselves.

Sometimes we suffer from the fact that the necessary exercise of fraternal charity, under this form of service, does not leave us more time for prayer and *lectio divina*. But if our heart is unified in God, we are also one with our brothers, and all the good that is accomplished in the community is ours; we pray with him who prays, and it is in his name that we work, for we are all one single body in Christ.

Chapter 6

BODILY ASCETICISM

1. The Meaning of Bodily Asceticism

Holiness does not consist in bodily penance. The sufferings and the hardship that we can impose on ourselves have by themselves no value in the sight of God. The motivation of Christian asceticism is to follow Christ. When Saint Paul wishes to give an explanation of the most profound meaning of the cross which the Master wants His disciples to carry, he writes in Philippians 2:5-8:

> Have in you the mind of Christ Jesus: he who, being God by nature, did not think that he should try by force to remain equal with God. Instead of this, he emptied himself, giving up his own free will, all he had, and took the nature of a servant. He became like man, appearing in human likeness. He humbled himself, making himself obedient unto death—his death on the cross.

Behind this text, it would seem, is the parallel with Adam and Christ familiar to Saint Paul (Rom 5:1-5). Adam had desired to seek equality with God as if by robbery, in disobedience to God's commandment. The evils which he had thus drawn down on his race were removed, by the humility, the obedience, the self-emptying of the Servant of the Lord.

Christ has thus opened the way for us to follow in his footsteps, as Saint Peter says (1 Pet 2:21). It is by this way that we have to go forward toward the purification of the heart of which Jeremiah speaks, the refashioning of our heart of stone into a true heart of flesh, in which Ezekiel saw the essence of the new and eternal covenant promised by both prophets.

It is, therefore, the love of Christ and neighbor, which should be the motivation of bodily mortification, not perverted self-love. Christ crucified needs to be expressed in bodily ascesis, so that, imprinted in our whole being, body and soul, this love may unify all their tendencies. Just as the concepts and reasonings of our discursive intellect need the embodiment of words, so also the love that dwells in our heart, in order to be expressed, to be deepened and to attain its full development, needs bodily gestures which symbolize it. Without this participation of the body, our spiritual life would run the risk of being merely a matter of beautiful ideas and of resolutions manufactured by the will instead of being the life of the heart, springing from the depths of our being recreated by grace. We shall succeed in destroying little by little the roots of our self-centeredness only if we cut out, generously and from the motive of love, a part of our bodily comforts. We can make certain spiritual attitudes truly our own only if we symbolize them by exterior practices and observances. Such is the function of the traditional "bodily exercises" of the monastic life.

2. The Great Laws of Asceticism

In order that the whole of the ascetical exercises involved in the life of the monk may fulfill this role, two conditions must be realized: that the exterior practices should be truly meaningful and perceived as such; and that they correspond to the measure of grace actually granted to the one who observes them, and also to the generosity of his response to this grace. An exterior practice, whose meaning escapes us entirely and whose exigencies really correspond to a spiritual love much higher than our own, cannot help the human and supernatural unification of our personality. A strained effort of the will may perhaps enable one to overcome the difficulty for some time, but the interior conflict will continue, and, if the observance in question holds an important place in the structure of our life, this conflict may one day break out into a grave crisis.

In order that an ascetical exercise, or some observance in general, may be truly meaningful, it is not necessary that it should

be capable of receiving an entirely rational justification, nor especially that the person concerned should have a clear knowledge
of this explanation. A simple and upright religious will be able
ordinarily to understand, as by instinct, the general meaning of
such a traditional observance and to embody in himself the corresponding interior attitude, without asking too many questions.

Such conduct is often more suited to prompting the true life
of the heart than the search for too great a rational clarity. On the
other hand, it is inevitable that many of the details of observance,
considered in isolation, may not be susceptible of a precise rational justification. Certain arrangements have no other purpose
than ensuring general discipline. Others have become obsolete in
the course of centuries, and no longer correspond exactly to their
original purpose. One could sometimes wish for some reforms,
but meanwhile a truly humble spirit will be able, without becoming stiff and wasting his energies in criticisms of detail, to find a
setup which remains as a whole quite adapted to the expression
of a true spirit of Christian ascesis and of contemplative prayer.

When it is a question of adopting measures that concern the
whole of a community, it will be evidently necessary to deter-
mine the happy medium. It must correspond not to an abstract
ideal, but to the real level of the whole, in such a way that there
is a margin for the generosity of the strong, who fulfill in the
monastic communities the role of a leaven, and that the weak
may not be discouraged, as Saint Benedict beautifully wrote
about the abbot:

> In his commands let him be prudent and considerate . . . bear-
> ing in mind the discretion of holy Jacob, who said: If I cause
> my flocks to be overdriven they will die in one day. Taking this,
> then, and other examples of discretion, the mother of virtues,
> let him so temper all things that the strong may have something
> to yearn for and the weak nothing to run from. (RB 64:17-19)

3. Bodily Exercises and Manual Work

Monastic tradition, from its origins until Cîteaux, has grouped
under the name of "bodily exercises" or "bodily labor" a whole

set of practices which constitutes the essential part of the ascesis of the monk.

Fasting, by checking the desire of earthly food, which symbolizes so well the rapacious tendencies of our fallen nature, helps the monk to open himself to spiritual realities and to revive in his heart the desire of heavenly nourishment, the Word of Life. Further, it enables him to practice almsgiving so that he distributes to poorer people what he has deprived himself of. Fasting constitutes a significant gesture of charity. In this matter, more than in all others, each one must know his measure. But it is essential that the fasting remains real and that we know how to impose on ourselves effective renunciation in the matter of food (quantity and quality).

Night watches, which are so favorable to the recollection of prayer, and which we devote to canonical vigils and to private prayer, inscribe in a bodily action the vigilance of the soul, its refusal to grow sluggish in the torpor of the forgetfulness of God and of His Word.

Deprivation of bodily comfort, by sleeping on a hard bed, or bearing cold and heat, is a witness to the preference given to the sweetness of God above the pleasant things of this life.

Without minimizing in any way the importance of these diverse forms of ascesis, "manual work should be given a special place among the bodily exercises." While certain monastic circles had shown some reserve in regard to manual work, for fear of compromising contemplative interiority or the abandonment to divine providence, the first Cistercians strongly insisted on its necessity. At the same time, they tried their best to effect a synthesis of all the elements contained in tradition, so that the exigencies of work might be combined harmoniously with those of the exterior and interior calm or quiet favoring contemplation.

In this perspective, manual work is first of all for the monk a necessity of the poverty which he professes. He must earn his bread by the sweat of his brow. As always in the matter of evangelical poverty, it is not the economic efficiency of the work that must first be considered here: the manual work, especially that which can be harmonized with the other exigencies of the monastic life, may not be the most "paying" for the monk. It may still be that which will help him the better to fashion for himself a poor heart.

There are other deep affinities between manual work and the monastic spirit. A work done seriously and with continued effort is an excellent preservative against the vice of acedia, sluggishness or disgust with spiritual things. It will help to discipline the tendency to instability of spirit and extroversion, and thus it will be an aid to contemplative recollection.

The physical fatigue produced by work enables the monk to express in his body his love of Christ crucified, and to imprint this love more deeply in his heart. The common works and humble tasks which do not earn for the one who does them any particular consideration in the community will help likewise to make humility penetrate our whole being.

Further, work is also an agent of psychological equilibrium for the contemplative. We must, however, avoid insisting on an exclusive fashion on this aspect, which is not the most essential. To make of work simply an element of relaxation in the life of the monk does not correspond to the meaning that tradition has given to it.

We must not, however, hide the real dangers which can be occasioned by manual work. It will always be difficult to maintain at a high spiritual level the whole of a community engaged in works of an absorbing nature. Some will incur the risk of allowing themselves to be led more by the rhythm of work than by their search for God, and if these cases are multiplied, the contemplative atmosphere will suffer from it.

A great vigilance is necessary if the diverse activities of the monastery are always to be regulated by a clear vision of the end to be pursued: union with God by the profound orientation of the heart toward Him alone.

Chapter 7

THE MONK'S PRAYER

1. Essence and Dimensions of Christian Prayer

Prayer is the expression of our spiritual life at its profoundest. And "so its sanctuary par excellence is our heart re-created by grace": it is from the heart that prayer must always proceed under its different forms.

In its essence, prayer is a simple attitude of the soul, a silent acquiescing to the action of the Holy Spirit who awakens in our heart a humble and suppliant desire of God and of the things of God. At the same time, it makes us experience a quiet and hidden joy and peace, giving us the conviction of being loved by our heavenly Father and of being continually saved by Him.

Even in its simplest expression, where it is reduced to a mere glance toward God, prayer assumes, in some sort, a passover rhythm: it is, on the one hand, the recognition and confession of our distress, of our inability to earn our true happiness by our own resources, confident supplication and filial self-surrender into the hands of the Father; on the other hand, it is the joyous confession of salvation already granted, thanksgiving and admiring praise. For it is by appropriating in us the prayer of Christ himself such as it sprang from his heart in His passion and His resurrection that the Holy Spirit teaches us to pray. For this reason, our prayer will correspond at the same time to that of the people of the Old Testament, whose existence was an announcement of the mystery of Christ. We ourselves know the groanings of slavery in Egypt, the foreign oppression and exile, but also the joyous thanksgiving and exultation caused by the "wonders" of great deliverances, which recall those of the first creation.

Moreover, if prayer truly proceeds from a heart animated by supernatural charity, it is accomplished in union with the whole Mystical Body of Christ. A Christian is never solitary in his action. The value of his prayer, in regard to God, is never derived from his personal fervor alone. If the Father accepts the prayer, it is because He sees in each suppliant His Son united to all His members.

2. Stages of the Life of Prayer

The different stages of the spiritual life were studied above. Let us come back to this subject here, and look at it from a more immediately practical point of view.

From the very beginning of the spiritual life, the Holy Spirit is present in the heart of the baptized person; He acts there and awakens prayer. But the soul remains too strongly attracted by sensible realities, to which it is drawn by the spontaneity of its nature, still infected by sexual desires and the need of controlling them, so that the divine attraction is not perceived by it. For thinking about God and about the things of God, for tending toward him, we have to make an effort which seems to us to go against the most natural tendency of our being.

Our prayer, instead of appearing to us as the expression of our deepest desire, is made up of acts which we force ourselves to produce, of reflections about truths expressed in words and concepts that remain exterior to us. It seems to us that all this activity proceeds from us alone, that we are entirely left to ourselves. Often, it is true, grace comes to our help by producing in the interior part of our soul a sensible emotion or some especially strong lights. But this sensible fervor, which can be the occasion of generous resolutions and of true progress, is still only a very imperfect sign of the presence of the Holy Spirit. It remains mixed with a subtle self-seeking which exposes us to the danger of becoming complacent about these consolations, of unconsciously preferring ourselves before others, of falling into the illusions of a false apostolic or reforming zeal, and it leaves us helpless when desolation follows later. A great openness with the spiritual father and a wise direction are indispensable here.

This active form of prayer is a stage that we have necessarily to go through. But from this period onwards, the beginner should be oriented toward the essential thing; he should be made to understand that our efforts of reflection, our sensible impulses, our detailed resolutions taken by means of the will, are not the principal part of prayer. Already the beginner can sometimes perceive, at a much deeper level, something of the divine instincts inscribed in his heart by the Holy Spirit; a desire of God which is extremely peaceful, sober, but which we suddenly feel is identified with our true self, that it represents what is dearest to our heart. Such moments of prayer are not the most consoling, but they are the truest and the most precious.

As the Holy Spirit gradually strengthens the hold these moments have on our being, and we become more deeply rooted in God, through our free will cooperating with grace, the dominant search for self-satisfaction is weakened in us, our heart is purified from its attachment to created things, which was preventing its steady progress, and we tend more spontaneously toward the good. We shall then come to realize truly that this profound tendency toward God, the presence of which we had sometimes felt in our heart, has become for us the essential thing, and that nothing else has any appeal for us anymore. In prayer, the exercise of the discursive intellect, and even the very simplified intuitions of our intelligence, the many affections and particular resolutions, appear as rather troublesome; one feels that the effort of the will that would be necessary for applying ourselves to these things would turn us away a little from that very simple glance toward God which alone is valuable to us.

Still, this profound attraction, whose existence we feel in a certain way in the most hidden depths of our heart, is not something sensible or something of which we are clearly conscious. We are not yet entirely possessed by God, and we have to make an effort for keeping our interior gaze turned quite simply toward God. The interior part of the soul is often subject to distractions, agitation, and trouble, though these do not gain access to the inmost sanctuary of the heart. This remains fixed in God, in a great peace; we suffer from these distractions, we know well that we should not be able to find our joy in any of these exterior things, and that, if we were to do it, the living water of prayer would at once cease to spring up in our heart.

It could subsequently happen that the divine ascendancy becomes stronger, more felt, more delightful. But the commonest condition of souls, whom a humble fidelity to grace has led to contemplative prayer—and there should be a good many of them in the monastery—is this prayer of pure faith, which is most often accompanied by an apparent dryness. This dryness, however, is not the aridity of a soul insensible to divine realities, but, on the contrary, the spiritual sobriety of a heart which experiences already a true intimate contact with God, such as can be achieved neither by the sensibility nor by the conceptual intellect.

What matters then is to persevere in this simple look toward God, using, if necessary, some formula of the barest kind—a mantra—which would then act as an evocation, awakening an echo in the heart, rather than offering a precise set of ideas to the intelligence. We might often have the impression of being inactive or of wasting our time. We might sometimes ask ourselves if we really pray; but Saint Anthony had this to say: "that prayer is not perfect where a monk understands his way and knows what he is praying." The best prayer is precisely that which leaves us altogether dissatisfied with ourselves and intensely resolved to give ourselves to God in the daily details of our life (which does not mean that we shall be preserved from faults of weakness, which are inevitable).

3. Liturgical Prayer and Private Prayer

The foregoing considerations on the nature and the stages of the life of prayer find their application both in our participation in the liturgy and in the exercise of private prayer. Far from being opposed, these two forms of prayer condition each other reciprocally; together they form a framework adapted normally to the development of a life of prayer, which will one day blossom into continual prayer.

The liturgy is at the same time a means of sanctification and worship. Under the first of these aspects, through the use of efficacious signs instituted by Christ or by the Church, the liturgy makes us participate in the saving mysteries of Christ, communicates His divine life to us, and thus unites us, in Him, to all the members of His Mystical Body. So far as it is worship addressed to God, it enables us similarly, by means of signs, to widen our prayer to the dimensions of Christ and His Church, and to make their intercession and their praise truly our own. Thus the liturgy is the privileged content of prayer and, for us, the source of all other forms of invoking God.

It is because the Christian's prayer has its roots in the liturgical celebration that, even when that prayer is performed by oneself, it is not purely private prayer, expressing only the sentiments of an individual and deriving all its value from the intensity of the personal devotion which inspires it; it is a truly common prayer in which the suppliant appears before God invisibly united with Christ and with His whole Mystical Body, and of which the theme is not different from the prayer of Christ Himself in His mystery of suffering and of glory.

But if private prayer must necessarily be *grounded* in liturgical worship, which is the highest of the two in dignity, the fruits of *liturgical prayer* themselves depend in a large measure on the fervor with which the participant devotes himself to *private prayer.* If participation in the liturgy is not prepared for, and prolonged through moments of private prayer, indispensable for a truly personal interior life, the liturgy is in danger of degenerating into an exterior and formalistic worship.

Finally, liturgical prayer and private prayer are themselves ordained to unceasing prayer. For this only means that our whole life is then perfectly dominated by the theological virtue of charity, which is the reality to which, in the present state of the Economy of Salvation, all the signs and all the exercises tend as to their final end.

4. The Component Parts of Liturgical and Private Prayer

If liturgical prayer and private prayer are to be harmonized and are to provide mutual enrichment, there should not be too great a divergence between the spirit and the disposition that are proper to the one and the other. If the life of prayer feeds exclusively on books of meditation and manuals of piety foreign to the spirit of the liturgy, it is much to be feared that private prayer will only lead to a sentimental devotion and that the liturgy, the Divine Office in particular, will only appear as a duty of which one acquits oneself out of a sense of responsibility. In such a case the celebration will not awaken any living echo in the soul. Such a dualism in the spiritual life of the monk will produce in him a profound uneasiness, and the result will be an unfortunate impoverishment.

It cannot be denied that modern methods of prayer can be a source of real profit to souls who feel attracted to them, if these methods are used with flexibility, in the spirit of the saints who created them. Still, for the sake of establishing a profound unity among the diverse elements of our spiritual life, we shall always find it advantageous to take our inspiration from the manner in which the ancient monks prayed. With them, liturgical prayer and private prayer were extremely close as regards the spirit, the structure and the contents, to the point of their nearly blending with each other. The one and the other involved the alternation of the three principal elements: reading, psalmody, prayer.

1. Reading. We spoke above of the importance, in the economy of our spiritual life, of hearing of the Word of God, and of the resonances that this Word awakens in the contemplative soul.

The liturgy contains readings, long or short, taken from Holy Scripture or from the commentaries of the Fathers. The *lectio divina* done in private will be in the nature of a prolongation of this liturgical proclamation. This exercise will have for nourishment Holy Scripture in the first place, and then other books that are profitable to the soul, that is to say, those that lead us spontaneously to prayer and recollection.

No doubt a more technical study of things divine should find its place in all monastic life, and of course the measure of it must vary considerably according to the aptitudes and needs of each one. This study will be pursued in an atmosphere of prayer and spiritual fervor; otherwise the theological reflection itself will remain a matter of speculation, instead of being more fertile by the sense of the mystery on which it is exercised, and of penetrating through the concepts to the divine realities.

Moreover, this intellectual work, even theological or biblical, should never be substituted entirely for *lectio divina* properly so called. It is most necessary that in the monk's daily routine there should be a place for slow, disinterested reading, exempt from all intellectual curiosity and penetrated by prayer, in which one is seeking only an encounter with God.

The study of divine truths and the *lectio divina*, centering round an assiduous and frequent use of the sacred texts, will imbue the monk little by little with the very ideals, images and even the terms of the Bible; consequently, a simple word, a passing allusion in a liturgical text, will suffice to kindle in his heart a burning spark of prayer, which will delight him and nourish him divinely.

2. Psalmody. The Psalms are admirably adapted to the expression of Christian prayer; there we find formulated in a powerfully suggestive manner all the great interior attitudes which Christ made His own and which He relives in us: confident supplication, self-surrender, self-less joy in the divine will, thanksgiving and praise.

That is why the Psalms constitute the essential ground of the Divine Office, especially of the monastic office. But it was not only in the liturgy that the ancient monks were praying with the Psalms. They were the principal nourishment and, as it were, the mold of their private prayer. This use of the Psalms in private prayer is very important; it can be a very efficacious factor of unity in our spiritual life, by bringing the life of prayer into full accord with liturgical piety. There is nothing anachronistic about imitating the ancient monks on this point.

It is not a question precisely of meditating on a psalm, by making it a subject of prayer around which one develops mentally a number of considerations, but of praying with a psalm, while following the text. This will be first of all for us a formula of prayer, which we must try to grasp by an effort of intellectual application, and by which we will try, painfully sometimes, to express something of the affections that we form in our own soul. But little by little this recitation will become more contemplative. For this it will be necessary to linger on a psalm, tasting it, lingering affectively for a long time on a verse that begins to awaken an echo in our heart.

It is this inmost echo, this silent response to the words of the prayer, a response that springs from the depths of our soul, that is here most important. It might be only a whisper hardly audible, but the soul should learn to become more and more attentive to it, till the words themselves are lost in interior silence.

It is moreover a familiar practice of the liturgy to use isolated verses of Holy Scripture which often keep coming back in the Office. Private prayer also can nourish itself during long moments by the loving repetition of a single verse that speaks to the heart. This way of praying with the help of a single verse ("monological" prayer) prepares us better for silent contemplation than does discursive meditation. It makes the soul simple, and habituates it to live in a spiritual poverty which is not indigence but the fullness of the life of the heart.

Obviously, the liturgical recital of psalms cannot have the freedom and spontaneity of the private use of them. But when properly prepared for, their liturgical use also admits of a great depth of contemplation. It is not really necessary, even at the Office, to force oneself to follow the meaning of each verse; it would be an excellent method of participating in the common prayer to find nourishment and self-expression in some verses gleaned here and there, which then continue to speak to our heart—a very simple interior occupation. In our monasteries, a contemplative soul, well trained, will generally experience no trouble in making the Office the normal framework of his prayer, while he would wish to be able to devote, outside of the liturgy, certain moments in like manner to a still more silent prayer.

3. *Prayer*. Liturgical prayer itself once included, after each psalm, a rather brief period of silence during which each one could pour out his heart before God in a quite spontaneous fashion; then the presiding minister of the assembly would raise his

voice for gathering together the prayer of all in a common prayer or "collect." The times of silence, which the liturgical celebrations still have, can be used in this way. Private prayer in particular must contain these effusions of the heart before God, brief of more prolonged as grace invites one to them. And little by little they will be transformed into those living moments of silence, in which prayer blossoms into contemplation.

It is to be wished that monks would learn to use a part of their time each day, especially the long intervals that separate the liturgical Offices on Sundays and feast days, entirely for the alternation of these exercises: *lectio divina* in the strict sense, rather than study; rumination (*meditatio*) of the Psalms or other similar texts; prayer leading to contemplation. It was thus that our Fathers lived.

Outside the content of prayer, there was another feature in all ancient monastic life that established a link between private prayer and liturgical celebrations: the frequent occurrence of the same bodily gestures, which often express better than words the profound attitudes of the soul. In the case of the first Cistercians themselves, private prayer was accompanied by bows or prostrations, brief and repeated, which, joined to a short invocation (the invocation of the Name of Jesus, of the Hail Mary) expressed contrition, compunction of heart, or simply veneration for the mystery recalled. Genuflection has the same meaning, while the standing position expresses the joyous and completely respectful attitude of the children of the resurrection who address themselves to their heavenly Father with a perfectly filial liberty and confidence (*parrhesia*). The sitting position favors contemplative attention. By the sign of the cross, which accompanies the more important formulae, like certain doxologies, the Christian in prayer stresses the fervor of his devotion and affirms the fullness of his personal adherence to the mystery recalled.

The practices now existing demand a greater sobriety in the gestures of private prayer. We must at least try our best to give to the different attitudes still used something of their meaning, instead of simply conforming ourselves to them by routine or by convenience.

5. The Guard over the Heart and Unceasing Prayer

The monks of old were really fascinated by the ideal of unceasing prayer proposed repeatedly by the New Testament: "We ought always to pray." They saw in this the aim of the monastic life here below. Some even drew an argument from this for counseling the monk not to be too attached to the feasts of the liturgical cycle, and to abstain from fixing, in the course of the day, particular times devoted to the celebration of the Divine Office: it is the whole life of the monks which ought to be a liturgy, and the fact of assigning fixed hours to prayer involves the danger of implying that one does not pray during the rest of the time. But subsequently, monastic tradition rather saw in the prayer of the Hours, which commemorate all through the day the great moments of the drama of redemption, the sign of the consecration of time in its entirety to God, a permanent reminder of our duty of unceasing prayer and a means of achieving it.

Unlike the liturgical Offices and the exercise of private prayer, unceasing prayer could not consist in explicit acts of prayer which one would be obliged to renew without ceasing. No doubt, such acts, brief but frequently repeated, will prepare the way for the grace of unceasing prayer. But essentially this does not consist in explicit acts. Unceasing prayer wears rather the aspect of an interior atmosphere which envelops the whole of life. It is much less a matter of the attention of the spirit than of the presence of the heart.

It is not a question of thinking about God always—our modern temperaments especially could hardly attempt this without being exposed to serious mental—but of doing all for God, following the impulse of His grace, without seeking ourselves. In order that our whole life may become prayer, it is not enough to do all our actions in the state of grace, nor even to offer them to God when we begin them: it is further required that all through our occupations we do not seek any other joy than that of pleasing God by responding to the good impulses that the Holy Spirit awakens in us, and this in a spontaneous fashion and almost without thinking about it. For, if for this we needed too much conscious effort and reflection, this would be a sign that our heart is not yet sufficiently pure, and its orientation toward God could not then maintain itselfon its precise course.

Unceasing prayer is, therefore, like contemplative prayer, of which it is only a diffuse form, the fruit of purity of heart. If our heart is pure, we seek only God in all things, and all our life becomes prayer. Each time that we are able to recollect ourselves more deeply, we shall be conscious not of resuming the course of a prayer interrupted over a period of time more or less long, but only of perceiving in a more explicit fashion the gushing forth of a living water which never ceases to spring up within us.

If our heart is divided, still encumbered with attachments to ourselves and to creatures, our prayer can only be discontinuous, and it will be characterized by constraint.

The only means of gaining access to unceasing prayer will, therefore, be to purify our heart, to rectify unceasingly the deep intentions which govern our activity. This is the goal of the exercise of Christian virtues and of all the practices of monastic ascesis. But these efforts themselves will be efficacious only if we avail ourselves of a strategy the for spiritual combat, which the ancient monks explained thoroughly. Saint Benedict summed up the essence of this in his chapter on the tools of good works: "When evil thoughts come into one's heart, to dash them at once on the rock of Christ, and to manifest them to an experienced spiritual father" (RB 4:50-51).

As a matter of fact, what corrupts the purity of our heart is the consent that we give to the evil suggestions that arise in us, and which incite us to seek our happiness in selfish satisfactions instead of placing it in God alone. It is these thoughts which are at the bottom of all sin. The chief activity of the monk consists in the invisible fight which he must carry on against them unceasingly—for unceasingly we are tempted to seek ourselves—so that he might keep his heart for God alone. This is indeed a formidable fight, a real crucifixion sometimes, in the arena of solitude where a man is no longer drawn out of himself by the luster of secular life.

We ought not to hide from ourselves the real dimensions of this fight: behind the evil tendencies which we are fighting is revealed the presence of personal adversaries—Satan and his

angels; their intervention in our life, under the form of evil suggestions, is undoubtedly a phenomenon much less rare than our
highly rationalistic mentality would incline us to suppose.

On the other hand, the only strength that enables us to triumph
over these germs of death is the love of God, the life of the risen
Christ which the Holy Spirit pours out in our hearts. The monk
thus relives, at the deepest level of his soul, Christ's own redemptive fight against Satan. It is Christ who, in him, will be a new
conqueror of the powers of evil.

In order to resist efficaciously the solicitations of the evil spirit,
we must first have a clear grasp of the "process of temptation."

The fathers have distinguished five principal moments: the
suggestion, the dialogue, the consent, the passion, the captivity.
The *suggestion* is the simple appearance in the consciousness
of an attraction for an evil action; this could be, for example, a
thought of vengeance, of gluttony, an invitation to give way to a
destructive sadness, and the like. It is involuntary, and it would
be vain to want to make sure that such impulses do not appear in
us; on the contrary, the temptation plays an important role in the
work of our sanctification by giving us the occasion of proving
our love. In the *dialogue* we reflect on the temptation and play
with it in some way. This may not involve any secret connivance
with the temptation, and may have no other purpose than that
of opposing contrary reasons to it. But this method is really quite
dangerous and is not ordinarily favored by the Fathers.

But hidden under the dialogue, there may already be a half-
consent, which is not entirely exempt from sin. The *consent* is a
personal decision and choice: we are content that our happiness
should consist in the evil enjoyment proposed to us; in some way,
we identify our deepest "self" with the evil tendency.

If such acts of consent are repeated, they give rise to the *passion*
or habit, which is like a second nature, and finally the *captivity*,
an irresistible impulse where liberty no longer plays any part.

If we wish to be on our guard against temptation, we must
know further the different forms under which it presents itself.
Saint John Cassian, following his master Evagrius, has drawn
up a catalog of all those evil thoughts which tend to make us

seek selfish satisfaction in the realities of this world, or to make us sad and irritated when we are deprived of them. All tradition has been influenced by this catalog, and the description that he gives of each item remains very appropriate, and can be of great profit to monks in our own day.

These evil impulses are greediness, lust, love of money (or desire to provide ourselves with a too-human security by the possession of certain resources), anger, evil sadness, *acedie* (or repugnance for the spiritual life and for ascetical practices), vainglory (seeking the approbation and the praise of others), and finally pride (by which we prefer ourselves to others and attribute to ourselves the good that is in us).

It is not always easy, however, to discover the exact nature of the impulses that arise in our heart. Satan knows how to transform himself into an angel of light. For discerning among our inspirations those which really come from the "good spirit" and those which proceed from the bad, the spiritual masters of the monastic life proposed quite early some rules for the "discernment of spirits," based on some very simple criteria which remain classic: an inspiration which leaves the soul in peace, without any impatience, stiffness or sourness of temper, has every chance of coming from the good spirit; on the contrary, trouble, stiffness, sourness, a bitter zeal, impatience, overexcitement of the imagination, a bigoted enthusiasm for abstract theories, are the ordinary signs that mark the presence of an illusion, a temptation under the appearance of good.

For exercising this discernment, there is need of a great purity of heart. Insofar as our heart is truly turned toward God, we shall feel, as by instinct, all that is out of tune with the atmosphere of peace which penetrates our soul. But if it still has too many affinities with evil, we shall be judge and defendant all in one, and our judgment shall be false. That is why tradition has always made of the manifestation of thoughts to a spiritual father, endowed with sufficient interior maturity, a cardinal point of the monastic method of spiritual formation. It is not a question merely of a confession of sins committed; this is equally necessary, no doubt, both because it constitutes an act of humility that purifies the soul, and because it lets the spiritual father know his disciple so as to be able to guide him efficaciously. But the essential purpose of the openness of conscience as understood by the monastic tradition is constituted by the thoughts, the diverse interior motions that solicit the soul and pose problems which, left to itself, it could not solve with security.

The role of the spiritual father here is to help the soul to become aware of the true significance of each of these inspirations, so that it can give a personal consent to the voice of the Holy Spirit when once this has been discerned.

As soon as the evil nature of a thought has been recognized, it ought to be fought against. It is better not to start a discussion with it, but to react right from the stage of the simple suggestion, without waiting till it has gathered strength and awakened complicity in our heart. Since the temptation manifests itself under the form of an attraction, only a greater love aroused in our heart by the Holy Spirit can enable us to triumph over it. And so the monk's chief weapon in this fight will be the untiringly repeated and confident recourse to the risen Christ, conqueror of Satan and of the world. It is thus that we ought to "catch the offspring of the devil, as soon as it has been formed in the thought, and dash it against the rock of Christ."

This invocation of Christ can assume various forms: a simple sign of the cross; a glance, purely interior perhaps, toward the crucifix, the true brazen serpent capable of healing us of the bite of the serpents of the desert; the verse *Deus in adjutorium meum intende*; the Jesus prayer: "Lord Jesus Christ, Son of God, have pity on me, a sinner"; the simple invocation of the Name of Jesus. The Lord will hear our prayer and respond to it by strengthening his love in our heart.

More and more, our prayer will interiorize itself, and come to be identified in some sort with this loving tendency itself; the result will be that we are rendered almost inaccessible to the suggestions of the Evil One. The monk will then always go deeper and deeper into this prayer now become unceasing, in which we have recognized the full accomplishment of the new creation of the heart inaugurated at baptism.

This is the announcement and the first fruits, for the entire Church, of the unfailing light of the world to come. Each Christian here below ought to strive to hasten its advent by carrying his own cross and by fidelity to his particular vocation.

PART THREE

THEOLOGY OF THE MONASTIC LIFE

Chapter 8

THE DEIFICATION OF THE CHRISTIAN

1. The Holiness and Nearness of God

> The Lord said to Moses, Speak to all the congregation of the
> people of Israel and say to them: You shall be holy, for I the
> Lord your God am holy. (Lev 19:2)

The basic meaning of "holy," which translates the Hebrew root
qds, is "separate." In usage, however, the word signifies divinity, the essence of deity itself. Holiness has been identified as
the numinous, the mysterious quality of the divine which is described as "the wholly other," that which strikes us with awe in
the presence of the Divinity. The effect of the numinous is twofold
and paradoxical. It is tremendous, fearful, but at the same time
it attracts and fascinates us: *mysterium tremendium et fascinasum.*
After wrestling at night with the angel of God and receiving his
blessing, Jacob exclaims: "I have seen God face to face yet I am
still alive!" (Gen 32:30).

God is holy, the entirely Other, the incomprehensible, the in-
effable, the inscrutable. No creatures, neither the angels nor the
saints in heaven, can comprehend God. Their knowledge of God
cannot be exhaustive; they share in the divine life, but this participation, though completely fulfilling, remains partial. Only the
Son and the Holy Spirit can sound the depths of God, because
they alone receive total communication from the Father and share
with the Father the unique divine essence, nature, being.

The spiritual and theological attitude of the Fathers of the
Church was profoundly marked by this sense of the inaccessibil-
ity of God. Monastic spirituality, particularly as requested in the

79

Oriental liturgies and very especially the Antiochean liturgical tradition, have always been particularly careful to safeguard the sense of the Divine Mystery against the exaggerated claims of human reason and a rationalistic attitude in our relation with God.

Father Bede Griffiths, in the introduction to *The Book of Common Prayer of the Syrian Church*, testifies to this when he writes:

> Undoubtedly, the chief characteristic of the Syrian liturgical celebrations is a sense of awe and wonder before the Divine Mystery. The Syrian liturgy is dominated by the scene of the vision of Isaiah, when he saw the Lord on a high and lofty throne in the temple, in Jerusalem, and heard the Seraphim— creatures of fire—before Him. In every Syrian church there is a curtain drawn across the sanctuary, recalling the curtain drawn across the sanctuary in Exodus, and the sanctuary itself is held to be the "holy of holies," the place where God Himself appears in the New Covenant with His people, acting in the Mysteries. This scene is recalled at the beginning and the end of every prayer service, so that the sense of wonder and mystery inspires and fills the whole liturgy (p. viii).

> Holy, holy, holy Lord, God of all cosmic forces.
> Heaven and earth are full of your glory.

In contrast with the Byzantine tradition, these acclamations are addressed to Christ:

> Holy are You, O God. Holy are You the Strong.
> Holy are You the Deathless who were crucified for us.
> Have mercy on us.

But the Holy God is also the God who is near. By his entirely free and gratuitous initiative, God has bestowed on the intelligent creatures he created in his own image and likeness a real, though necessarily limited, participation in his divine nature. Obviously there is no unity of essence in this case but only free union of wills. We are united, one with God, even here below, when, like Jesus of Nazareth, we do God's will: "I have come, not to do my own will, but the will of Him who sent Me" (John 5:30).

However, this distinction does not reduce the deification of the believer to a simple metaphor or an imagined likeness. On the contrary, this transformation was understood by the early Fathers of the Church, and after them by the Cistercian Fathers of the twelfth century, in an extremely realistic sense, which nevertheless safeguards the absolute transcendence of God.

In this union the created will and the divine will do not remain exterior to each other, as if the human will conformed itself to the divine will in a purely moral fashion, by the pure exercise of freedom in the observance of the commandments. By the grace of God, the work of the Holy Spirit, the relation or communication which is supremely free, the divine activity becomes, as it were, "interior" to the believer's most personal activity; it penetrates it so deeply that it transforms and deifies it. The human will is then vitally united with the will of God in love. It is this which prompts Saint Bernard to say, following the tradition, that the human soul is *capax Dei*, "capable of receiving God." As a vessel has the capacity of containing one liter of milk, the human soul has the capacity of becoming united with God:

> I pray that they may all be one, as You Father are in Me, and I in You. (John 17:23)

> I am the vine and you are the branches. He who abides in Me and I in him, he it is that bears much fruit. (John 15:5)

This may be better understood in relation to Saint Bernard's teaching on the degrees of love:

1. In the first degree the human being loves himself for his own sake, for his own gratification; everything is centered on himself. In fact, here there is no love of God, only of self.

2. In the second degree he begins to love God because good things come from God. He loves God for his own benefit, his own advantage, for the favors he obtains from Him.

3. In the third degree of love, having more frequent recourse to God, he discovers how good and sweet God is. He begins to love God for God's sake.

When my heart was embittered, I did not understand
Yet I was always with you,
You were holding me by my right hand.
You guide me by Your counsel and so lead me to glory.
What else have I in heaven but You?
Apart from You I want nothing on earth.
My body and my heart faint for joy.
God is my possession for ever.
I wish to draw near to God.
Be good to me, Lord my trust,
that I may recount all your wonders. (Ps 73:21-28)

4. This God experience of the psalmist shows us how we attain the fourth degree of love, when man loves himself only
for the sake of God. He gives himself unconditionally and
totally to God, as Jesus Himself indicated when He said, "no
one has greater love than this, to lay down his life for his
friends" (John 15:13). To lay down one's life does not mean
necessarily to sustain death, but to dedicate oneself totally
and unconditionally in surrender to the divine will.

> "I came not to do My own will," said Jesus, "but to do the
> will of him who sent Me. My food is to do the will of him
> who sent Me." (John 4:34)

Here is how Saint Bernard explained the fourth degree of love to
his monks. He summed up the first three degrees in one sentence:
"The satisfaction of our wishes, our success in life, now delights
us less than to see the will of God done in us and for us, as we
pray so often: 'Your will be done on earth as it is in heaven.'"
He then proceeds with the fourth degree, starting with a prayer:

> O pure and sacred love! O sweet and pleasant disposition of
> the heart! O pure and sinless intention of the will, all the more
> sinless and pure since it frees us from selfish vanity, all the more
> sweet and pleasant, because all that is found in it is divine. It
> is deifying to go through such an experience.

And the experience is described by analogies:

As a drop of water seems to disappear completely in a big quantity of wine and even assumes the wine's taste and color; as the red-molten iron becomes so much like fire that it seems to lose its primary state; as the air on a sunny day seems to be transformed into sunshine, instead of being lit up; so it is for the saints, that all human concerns melt in a mysterious way and flow into the will of God. Otherwise, how can God be all in all (1 Cor 15:28) if we are still ruled by human concerns? No doubt the substance remains, but under another form, another glory, another power.

Here Bernard bursts into prayer:

When will this happen? Who will see it? Who will ponder it? When shall I come and appear in God's presence? O my Lord, my God! My heart speaks of you. It says: Seek his face. It is your face, Lord, that I seek. (*On Loving God*, 28)

This deification was conceived by the Fathers as the restoration of the divine image and likeness in which our first parents were created, but which was lost at the Fall on account of disobedience, misuse of God's gift of freedom. Lost at the Fall, it is, however, restored, fully accomplished in Jesus of Nazareth, the Christ, by the union of His humanity with the divine nature, in the Person of the Word of God, without confusion or mixture. From Him we come to share in it.

2. Supernatural, Mystical Anthropology

The place where this deification takes place is the heart of the believer, in which the love of God—the God who is love—"is poured into our hearts by the Holy Spirit" (Rom 5:5). The human "heart" is understood in the sense which the Bible and the Fathers give to this word. It does not refer to any emotion of a sensible and superficial nature. It is, rather, the deep seat of true knowledge as well as of love. It is thus better understood as a religious experience, a God-experience. "He who loves, is born of God and knows God. He who does not love does not know God; for God is love" (1 John 4:7). The "heart" thus refers to mind, soul, spirit and one's entire emotional nature and understanding. It is for all these reasons that it must be considered as the center and source of man's deepest inclinations, those that bring it about that he thinks, speaks and acts spontaneously in such and such a manner.

That we were created in the image and likeness of God implies that our heart is made for God. It is only in God that humanity's fundamental tendency toward happiness can find its fulfillment. Nevertheless, this profound attraction for God, and the inborn sense of what is spiritually good, become fully efficacious and receive their supernatural character only when the heart is re-created by the work of the Holy Spirit.

One of Bernard's most deeply rooted beliefs was that human beings have by nature (i.e., by God's gift at creation) an innate capacity and tendency which moves the whole being in the direction of God. There is therefore an innate spirituality. Religion is not an optional extra, but the flowering of a universal potentiality without which it is impossible to be fully human. Not to seek God is an act of self-destruction, the ultimate tragedy, whereas to find God is also to find oneself, to experience something of the boundlessness of our being in the transcending of our familiar limitations.

But all is grace. It is not a matter of human achievement, but of the human will giving assent to God's will manifested in our life's circumstances. For this, one must be trained to recognize the deceptive and ephemeral character of all that is not God. Then only can one progressively give oneself to what is true. There be an aversion to material things before a progressive must conversion toward the realm of the spirit, of the heart, to God can take place:

> God sent His own Son in the form of sinful flesh. He condemned sin in the flesh, in order that the just requirement of the law might be fulfilled in us, who walk not according to the flesh but according to the Spirit. Those who live as the Spirit tells them to, have their minds controlled by what the Spirit wants. To be controlled by the flesh (human nature) leads to death; to be controlled by the Spirit results in life and peace. (Rom 8:3-6)

Without grace, the work of the Holy Spirit in us, our inner inclinations toward the good remain incapable of resisting our self-centered, selfish tendencies, seeking satisfaction in created, worldly goods, none of which can fulfill. After his confession of Jesus' divinity, Saint Peter was taught this, as our Lord said: it is not flesh and blood which revealed this to you, but my Father in heaven (Matt 16:17). Yet soon after this, when hearing for the first time Christ's prediction of his passion, Peter, according to his temperament, protested vehemently: "God forbid, Lord! This shall never happen to You." Then received Christ's most sharp rebuke: "Get away from Me, Satan, you are a stumbling block to Me, your mind is not on things divine but on human things" (Matt 16:23).

Such enslavement to one's "self" is not connected only with our lower nature, as bodily gratification, gluttony, drinking, and sexuality, but also with seeking self-satisfaction in social life, and even in the religious life, whenever we indulge in priding ourselves, in dominating, in intolerance, in seeking the first places, in contempt for those who do not share our views. All these are matters which have to be first acknowledged, then also corrected. Attention to this will refine our conscience and lead us to purity of heart, so often recurring in our prayer, the eighth beatitude mentioned in the Sermon on the Mount: "Blessed are the pure in heart, for they shall see God." In the neglect of this acknowledgement there is a lack of the two fundamental virtues of reverence and humility.

Consequently, the original unity of human love—love of God and neighbor—is broken into a multitude of desires foreign to our deepest nature. This rupture of our interior unity introduces into us the germ of spiritual death. At the same time our union with the whole creation is broken. As Paul wrote to the Romans:

> The creation waits with eager expectation to see the manifestation (the revealing) of the children of God. (Rom 8:19)

On the contrary, in the measure in which the Holy Spirit accomplishes His life-giving work in the heart of the believer and restores its purity, the original unity of creation is recovered. When we free ourselves from our self-centered feelings and behavior, from the isolation of our sinful condition, we become conformed to the creative intention of God. This is the theme of return to paradise cherished by the Fathers.

At the same time, we receive the pledge of the eschatological condition of humanity delivered from its present animal condition and we are introduced among the angelic choirs. This is the theme of the angelic life so prominent in the Antiochean liturgy. In this way, the distorted divine image is being restored to the likeness of God.

Already here below, the Divine Life exercises its mastery over the body itself, correcting its sensual tendencies. While the body remains subject to suffering and death, it experiences already the firstfruits of the final transfiguration.

It is of the highest importance to realize that the spiritual life is essentially the life of the heart re-created by the Holy Spirit. What gives authoritative guidance to spiritual persons are neither the spiritual impulses, however generous, of their sensibility, nor the certitudes acquired by reason and the discursive intellect, even enlightened by the data of faith. Such persons are prompted and guided by the inner attractions and instincts engraved in their hearts by the Holy Spirit which, far from frustrating the spontaneous movements of our true nature, fulfills its deepest aspirations beyond all expectations.

Assuredly, these instincts of grace—works of the Holy Spirit in us—if they are authentic, must always be in perfect agreement with the teaching and directions by the custodians of divine authority. But if the Spirit does not speak within, we profit nothing by the truth that is proposed to us from outside.

Therefore, the believer who wishes to make progress is not asked to work up a large fund of sensitive enthusiasm and persuasive considerations to construct his love for God and his orientation toward the good. Above all, it is a question of discovering these tendencies which are secretly present and active, of letting them take possession of our whole being, little by little, and of integrating our sentiments and desires.

Thus, all in all, the growth in the spiritual life can be described as a return to one's heart. It is by such a return that conversion begins. Like the prodigal son, the sinner "enters into himself." And this is true not only of a conversion from sinful life, but also of a new turn taken in life—sometimes at a time of trial. Of Saint Benedict, it is narrated in his life by Saint Gregory the Great that when he discovered that the monks of Vicovasa, who had called him from his hermitage to be their abbot, had tried to poison him, "he went back to the wilderness he loved, *to live alone with himself in the presence of the Heavenly Father.*" Without going away to a hermitage, the monk must take care every day to make a place in his life for moments of meditative reflection to return to his heart, to enter into himself, to be alone with God.

As for the sinner, he becomes conscious of the abyss of his misery, of the interior tearing and rending from which he suffers. In the Acts of the Apostles, it is said that after hearing Peter's exhortation on the day of Pentecost, the people "were pricked in their heart" (2:37). None of the created goods in which the new convert sought happiness is capable of filling the void of a heart made for God. The experience of this interior void reveals, negatively, the truth about being made in the image of God. As the features of the divine resemblance are gradually restored interiorly, it is again by entering into his heart, illumined by the divine presence, that the convert will experience the truth of the divine pardon and acquire a knowledge of God that tastes sweet and radiates gently: the pledge and firstfruits of the Spirit—the love, joy and peace of eternal life.

3. The Redeeming Economy

By Adam's fall into sin human nature was deprived of its true life, the eternal life with which it was originally endowed. However, the image of God was not entirely destroyed in us; we retained our freedom; we remained *capax Dei*, radically capable of receiving God, of consenting freely to God's will. But this fundamental capacity could be actualized hereafter only through a free initiative of the merciful God.

It is by the cross and the resurrection of Christ that humanity was restored to its condition of divine sonship. By becoming incarnate, God took upon Himself suffering and death, and triumphed over them.

Christ made suffering and death the expression of His filial love and of His perfect obedience to His Father. Risen and exalted at the right hand of God, He sends us His Spirit, who re-creates our hearts whenever He meets with a free response. When our will joins and cooperates with the will of God, we are enabled to convert the cross, suffering and death into expressions of that love which gives us the strength to prefer the will of our heavenly Father to all earlier pursuits or achievements. As Jesus Himself said: "I came, not to do my own will but to do the will of him who sent Me." "My food is to do the will of Him who sent Me and to accomplish His work" (John 6:38; 4:34). These words have a special resonance for monks. When they do the will of God, they do also the work of God; their whole life can rightly be described as doing the work of God.

By His cross, our Lord offered to His Father a perfect sacrifice for the salvation of the world. He conquered Satan, who had been holding humankind captive, and He has given us, creatures made out of dust, the perfect proof of His love for us. The believer who takes up his cross and follows the Lord is also making of his life a liturgy to the glory of the Father and for the salvation of the world; he triumphs over Satan by returning love for love.

But it is the Holy Spirit who conforms us to Christ in the mystery of His death and resurrection. It is the Spirit who makes the plenitude of the new life available to each person. He is the love of the Father for the Son and the love of the Son for the Father in the bosom of the Holy Trinity. In the temporal mission on which He is sent by Christ, the Holy Spirit becomes the love of God for us and our love for God. While it is true that the contemplation of the redemptive suffering of our Lord gives us the supreme motivation for loving God, the Holy Spirit poured forth into our hearts is the love with which we love God.

This deifying action of the Holy Spirit is adapted to the diversity of persons. It is the unique life of the risen Christ that He makes available to each one, but He adapts this action to the innumerable variety of spiritual personalities, each saint being a unique personality. The harmonious combination of the different charisms, given to teach for the utility of all, reminds us that the Church, the Body of Christ, is a living organism—not simply a legal organization.

Further, it must not be forgotten that the Virgin Mary, Mother of God, is the most perfect example of this life in Christ. When the Holy Spirit overshadowed her and she gave her assent, she conceived Him and became the source of divine life in us. Through her, Christ comes to be born and grows in us; God made the Blessed Virgin Mary a perfect mirror of the uncreated wisdom whom she was privileged to carry in her womb. The Lord was pleased to confer on her all the partial perfections granted to the other creatures. As the new Eve, associated with the new Adam, it was granted to her to participate in the whole of Christ's work of salvation. In him and by him, through the work of the Holy Spirit, she has become the source of Divine Life always springing up. It is through her unique participation, as source, in the life of Christ that all graces come to us. Consequently, veneration of and love for the Blessed Virgin Mary is at the heart of the life of the monk. Close to her, tradition has placed John the Baptist, the immediate forerunner and instrument of the baptism of Jesus, culminating in the proclamation of His Divine Sonship. At the beginning of the *Qurbana*, our eucharistic celebration, the celebrant addresses Jesus, referring to the intercession of both Mary and John: "May Mary who brought you forth and John who baptized you be intercessors on our behalf."

4. Sacramental Grace and Personal Effort

The foundation of our life in Christ is the sacrament of baptism or, more exactly, the three sacraments of Christian initiation taken together: baptism, chrismation and Eucharist, which are still conferred together at baptism in the Malankara Church, contrasting the Roman practice of conferring them separately.

By baptism, the old nature in us is put to death, as our whole being is taken possession of by the risen Christ. Baptism delivers us from the dominion of Satan. It makes us die to the world and

to the flesh while introducing us into the liberty of the children
of God.

Chrismation sets the seal of the Holy Spirit on the newly baptized. The grace conferred by this sacrament is the communication of the gifts of the Holy Spirit. His own life and love are given
in view of the spiritual warfare that the believer must carry on
in the Church, through a life of self-denial, with a view of sharing with the needy, in witnessing to Christ's work of salvation.

The purpose of the Eucharist is to nourish our spiritual life by
actuating in the Church Christ's work of salvation, His redeem-
ing sacrifice. Eucharist means "thanksgiving offering." While
offering *Qurbana*—thanksgiving to God—the Body and Blood
of Christ are given to the believer who participates in the celebration. This leads him into a life-giving communion with Him.
Further, the Eucharist is also the prefiguration and efficacious
sign of the consummation of the mystical marriage, the union
of the Church and of each believer with Christ.

Yet, the grace of the sacraments is not a substitute for one's
own personal effort. On the contrary, grace calls for personal
cooperation, awakens it and sustains it. The sacraments do not
give us the new life as a gift ready-made for enjoyment. Their
role is to be compared to a seed that must sprout up, and bears
fruits only in good soil.

The believer must, therefore, take up his cross and follow
Christ, in order to realize the sacramental mystery personally,
by consenting freely to the invitations of the divine love poured
forth into his heart by the Holy Spirit. When the believer accepts
suffering and death willingly, and not merely submits to them
out of necessity, he makes of them the sign of his renunciation
of all self-centeredness, and of his filial love for the heavenly
Father. In this way the mystery of death and of life into which
he has been initiated in the sacramental celebration enters more
and more deeply into the details of his everyday life.

This daily cross will be made up of the trials and failures,
setbacks and reversals of progress due to human nature and
allowed by Providence. Among these are the following: the ago-
nizing fight against persistent temptations, the purification of the

sensibility—our feelings—and of the intelligence, without which one cannot attain to spiritual sobriety and purity of contemplation. And, for the monk, the cross also includes the practice of the great evangelical counsels and all the demands of asceticism.

A true understanding of the cross—the intimate conviction that the light of Christ's resurrection, revealed only to the eyes of faith, is present in the midst of suffering—can give meaning to the life of the monk, as also to the sacrifice of the martyr.

5. The Word of God and Spiritual Life

Among the real and always available sources of our spiritual life, Holy Scripture, received into the Church and upheld by her tradition, must be placed beside the mysteries of Christian worship. Indeed, part of them.

The Word of God, living and life-giving, is supremely important for the education of the heart. As a matter of fact, the sacraments or mysteries produce in our hearts the divine instincts, which are the law of the Spirit which Jeremiah prophesied: "I will put my law in them and write it upon their hearts" (Jer 31:33, quoted at length in Heb 8:10). In this light all our activities ought to be guided by the Holy Spirit, beginning with our thoughts. But these instincts are not readily perceived by our conscience. Moreover, we ought to be able to refer them always to an objective law or tradition which authenticates them. As Saint Peter wrote, "We have been born anew, not of perishable but imperishable seed, through the living and enduring Word of God" (1 Pet 1:23).

The Word of God, proposed by the Church, is precisely this norm, by which the believer must always measure his conduct. In the epilogue of his Rule, Saint Benedict, pointing to the height of perfection for the monk, exclaims with zest: "For what page or what utterance of the divinely inspired Books of the Old and New Testaments is not the most true rule for human life?" (RB 73:3).

Yet it is not enough to conform ourselves to it as to a purely exterior authority. The Word of God must penetrate deeply into our being, and keep resounding in our heart, so that under its impact the divine instincts of which we wrote above may be awakened, little by little, and our activity may be inseparably the fruit of our listening to the exterior precept and of our docility to the interior inspiration.

That is why the ancient monastic tradition regarded unceasing rumination of the Word of God as one of the principal supports of the monastic quest and self-discipline. It has always looked upon Holy Scripture, especially the Gospels, as the chief and, in a sense, the universal and sole rule of the monk.

Chapter 9

THE GROWTH OF THE LIFE IN CHRIST

1. The Active Stage of the Spiritual Life

Baptism delivers us from the captivity of Satan, but does not suppress in us concupiscence, which is mainly sexual desires, but also the desire of worldly things as they are proffered in our media and our consumer culture. As a disorderly attraction toward sensual, selfish enjoyments, concupiscence is opposed to the virtue of temperance. The four traditional cardinal virtues in classic Catholic theology are prudence, justice, fortitude, and temperance, whose specific work is to assure the mastery over the instincts: "Do not follow your lust, keep your passion under control" (Sir 18:30). In the baptized Christian the desires for the pleasures of this world no longer have the compelling character of the law of sin, which draws the unredeemed person irresistibly toward evil.

The Holy Spirit, who dwells in the heart of the baptized, awakens in us a supernatural attraction toward God and the things of God, which fortifies us against the seductions of self-love and sensual pleasures and enables us to resist them, and eventually to overcome them. Yet, we should not forget that this is a lifelong struggle, a spiritual warfare.

Indeed, during the early stages of one's training for spiritual growth, the attraction for the things of this world still remains very strong, because the promptings of the Holy Spirit take place in depths so hidden that the soul hardly becomes conscious of these motions.

Generally, the divine will appears to the new monk rather as a law which is imposed on him from outside and to which he has to submit himself by doing violence to his spontaneous tendencies, which remain disorderly. He cannot say like Jesus, "My food is to do the will of Him who sent Me and to complete His work" (John 4:34).

In spite of the presence within him of the Holy Spirit, acting in a hidden manner, the believer is still, on the level of psychological consciousness, at a state when the hope of a reward—the second step of love of God, according to Saint Bernard, when the believer loves God primarily in the hope of a reward or the expectation that his good deeds will be seen by his companions—plays an important role. The change to a more spontaneous striving often comes at a time of crisis, when he becomes aware of the futility of his life. This is no longer a coercion from outside, but an interior call, an interior prompting which materializes in a vocation and in following a life of dedication.

At that time, it often happens that the Holy Spirit awakens in the beginner a sensible fervor which will help him in the spiritual warfare. But this fervor, like the movements of the sensible order, lacks stability, and has about it something of an accidental, nonessential nature in relation to real love. Moreover the withdrawal of such graces is part of the divine pedagogy. It helps toward establishing the soul more firmly in the life of virtue and in making it pass from the state of sensible love to a more and more spiritual love.

This is also the meaning of trials by temptation, whatever be the form they assume. These forms vary much according to the personal character of the monk: temptations of the flesh, difficulties of obedience, dissatisfaction at a perceived lack of opportunity, apparently unjust treatment affecting the development of one's natural talents, loneliness under all its forms, the *acedia* or apathy of the Desert Fathers, weariness of heart which makes one lazy, sluggish, and slothful. On the other hand, when one is talented and excels in the fulfillment of all his official duties, he is exposed to temptations of vanity, accompanied with intolerance of others' views, which leads to arrogance and even to fanaticism. These are the antipodes of the reverence, humility and love which constitute the good soil where the seed yields in one case a hundredfold, in another sixty, and in another thirty

(Matt 13:23), though patience and endurance are also required for this (Luke 8:15).

Such trials can indeed be turned to good when they produce in the monk the consciousness that, after all, he remains a sinner, as well as when they help to detach him from his natural activity, which is still subject to the consequences of sin. It is in this way that the believer is taught gradually to live above all for God, for God alone, to live more and more by faith, entirely dependent upon God's granting His grace. It is when we willingly commit ourselves to God's love and his all-powerful grace that real renewal—the new life—takes place in us; in God's own time and in His own way, we see the "wonders" that were once realized in Jesus and His saints.

2. Purity of Heart, Aim of the "Active Life"

If the monk tries hard and generously to do the divine will in spite of repugnance to a particular work or situation, while trusting in the divine help, little by little the Holy Spirit will strengthen the monk's hold over his own being, and the practice of virtue will become for him easier and more spontaneous, as Saint Benedict observes in the conclusion of his important chapter on the Ladder of Humility:

> No longer will his motive be the fear of punishment, but rather the love of Christ, good habit and delight in the virtues which the Lord will deign to show forth by the Holy Spirit in his servant now cleansed from vice and sin. (RB 7:68-69)

He will discover in doing the divine will a profound joy, quiet and hidden, which will strengthen him against evil tendencies and the suggestions of Satan, in a manner much more efficacious and permanent than fear or hope or purely sensible fervor.

The practice of virtue will become, as it were, natural for him. He then embraces it "for the love of Christ," as Benedict says, and "for love of virtue," as Cassian puts it. The two expressions are equivalent. For the Fathers, virtue or the good are not abstract ideals or simple moral perfection. They are a person, the Lord

Jesus such as we contemplate Him in each page of the Gospels. What we call charity, gentleness, humility, chastity and the like are concretely nothing else than the life of Christ in us. "Abide in Me and I in you. As the branch cannot bear fruit by itself, unless it abides in the vine, neither can you, unless you abide in Me" (John 15:4). Similarly, the joy that the purified heart experiences in the pursuit of these virtues under the impulse of the Holy Spirit is actually an authentic experience of the sweetness of Christ present in us (see Matt 11:25-30).

This spontaneity and this stability in the practice of virtue—though still subject to ups and downs—is marked by true humility. Spiritual persons remain conscious of frailty. They feel clearly that all this is a gift of God, having no proportion to their own effort. This points to the culmination of the active life. It signifies the rectification of the passions (*apatheia*), purity of heart, the Sabbath or rest of the new creation of the soul, and perfect love or charity.

3. Contemplation and Spiritual Sobriety

"Blessed are the pure in heart, for they shall see God" (Matt 5:8). Purity of heart, which is traditionally considered as the second stage of the spiritual life, is the gate of the contemplative life, the ultimate stage. When love is well awakened and active in the heart, our knowledge of God surpasses in some way the recourse to reason, to notions and concepts acquired by the intellect. Some very simple souls, sometimes even psychologically unbalanced, (for example, Saint Benedict Joseph Labre, who was found unfit by both the Trappists and the Carthusians) have reached the highest degree of Divine Love.

In accord with the fundamental affirmations of our faith, this is something that is experienced in the heart. God is love, and the love poured forth into our heart enables us to experience in ourselves something of the inclinations of His heart: "Everyone who loves is born of God and knows God, for God is love" (1 John 4:7).

Christian contemplation is not, therefore, some superior kind of intellectual knowledge. It is an experience of the deifying presence of Christ and the Spirit in us. Thus, the ancient monastic Fathers speak frequently, in this connection, of interior sweetness, of affections, of fruition or enjoyment.

This spiritual experience is of quite a different order from the sensible consolations of beginners. This is why the spiritual writers put the emphasis on spiritual sobriety and express themselves with great caution on the subject of visions, revelations, and, in a general way, of all those forms of religious exaltation originating in a sensibility which has not yet been radically re-created by the Holy Spirit.

4. The First Manifestation of Contemplation

A first manifestation of contemplation consists in the way in which created realities are considered by the soul that has been profoundly purified and integrated and appears calm, quiet.

In general, the monk whose heart has been purified penetrates, as it were, instinctively beneath the surface of things, the purely human attraction they have, so that he discovers God in them and tastes God in them. Instead of awakening in him a desire for selfish enjoyment, all creatures speak to him of the love which God has for all and for him. He is possessed of a kind of supernatural instinct by which he is enabled to discover the Creator's intentions, as they are expressed in nature, and to perceive the finger of God in the course of events.

To the gaze of the pure in heart, through the power of the risen Christ and of the Holy Spirit, the world becomes, as it were, an immense burning bush, manifesting the glory of God. By his ascetic practice, the monk liberates creation from the futility to which it has been subjected against its own will, "not by its own choice" (Rom 8:20). He transfigures it by the cross planted in his own life. And, by thus offering it mystically in sacrifice, by his own renunciation, he restores in Christ the cosmic liturgy of which the First Adam was destined to be the priest. In this light, the monk's vocation is a call to a spiritual priesthood in contrast with the ministerial priesthood ordained for the sacramental life of the Church.

When reading Holy Scripture, the monk does not stop at the historical and episodic shell of past events. He actualizes the Word by discovering that it is addressed to him personally and is thus ever real and relevant. In the history of the people of God, he reads the history of God's interventions in his own life, linked to that of the whole Church.

5. Pure Prayer and Unceasing Prayer

In what Saint John Cassian calls "pure prayer," the monk is taken hold of by God in a profound manner. He experiences the intimate presence of God beyond all interior speech and in the silence of images and concepts. Consequently he is already, as it were, ravished out of this present world and he tastes the firstfruits of the eternal beatitude.

The ancient monastic Fathers, such as Isaac of Nineveh, frequently associate the gift of tears. With this experience, which, in its fullness, is granted only to a very small number of souls. Tears, silent and quiet, do not proceed from any superficial stirring of the sensibility, but bear witness to the transfiguration of one's whole being by the work of the Holy Spirit. This baptism by the Holy Spirit gives experimental assurance of the perfect purification of the soul, and manifests the full flowering of these divine realities of which the first image was presented by sacramental baptism, which at the same time conferred the seed of future growth.

The re-creation of the heart by the Holy Spirit produces more than a passing experience, however luminous. It leads the monk finally to a state of constant prayer. The dominating influence of love in the heart becomes so profound and so universal that all its actions and all its attitudes proceed spontaneously from love.

As Origen taught, the whole of life then becomes prayer, since it is entirely oriented toward God, without any indulgence in self-centered, selfish love, so far as this is attainable or possible to human weakness. The heart, seat of our deepest being, then becomes what it was before the Fall: a place of perpetual liturgy in which prayer goes on without ceasing. In the case of a small number of souls, this prayer maintains them in the loving remembrance of God, even through the most diverse occupations. The Syriac Fathers often refer to the "altar of the heart" on which the monk celebrates an unceasing liturgy.

6. The Law of Unceasing Progress

Among the different stages of the spiritual life, as sketched above, there is no need to establish any sharp distinctions. It is not so much a question of successive stages as of different aspects of a vital growth. What must be remembered above all is that, on the one hand, intimate union with God, "contemplation," presupposes the long spiritual warfare of the active life and that, on the other, our life in Christ is essentially a matter of growth. What really matters is to try not to measure the way that has been covered, so as to feel either satisfaction or discouragement, vainglory or impatience. What our Lord demands of us every day, at each instant, is to begin to serve him, persuaded that we have accomplished nothing yet: a perpetual beginning again, with unwearying confidence in the mercy of the Lord and the victorious power of his Resurrection and Pentecost. Such is all the perfection which the monk is called to strive after and to tend in this life.

EPILOGUE

With the help of our Lord, we have completed this systematic exposition of the early Cistercian monastic tradition, which was born of an earnest and long-tested desire to recover an authentic and fervent practice of Saint Benedict's Rule for Monks, understood as a close discipleship of Christ.

The early documents which the founders have left us witness, above all, to their desire for a genuine, and even austere, monastic way of life. They described themselves as "poor with the poor Christ." They renounced all revenues coming from outside and made their livelihood by their own labor. They distanced themselves from the world not only by withdrawing to solitary places, but also by committing themselves not to be entangled in earthly matters in order to occupy themselves with heavenly affairs.

It was this which prompted the second generation led by Saint Bernard to set out on their spiritual quest at three levels: the quiet of the cloister, the quiet of the mind and the quiet of contemplation. This was pursued in an intense community life. They were known as "lovers of the brothers and of the place": "Since they were of one heart and one soul, and held all things in common, there was concord and unity throughout, for they were always putting the common good before their own individual convenience" (John of Ford). Here we have a clear echo of the last chapter of Benedict's Rule: "On the Good Zeal Monks Ought to Have."

About Saint Bernard's own formation at Cîteaux, we hear a good deal in the *Vita Prima* (chap. 8):

> Because he desired to lead the common life to the full, when
> his brothers were engaged in some manual work which he

could not undertake . . . he used to do his share of work for the house by digging, chopping wood, or carrying materials for the others to use in their work, or doing any of the more wearisome but unskilled jobs. And if he found that he was not strong enough to do these, he used to find himself even more menial tasks to do. In this way he made up for his incapacity for work by his great humility.

The grace and help which he found in the contemplation of the things of God enabled him not only to put up with such tiring little jobs, but even to enjoy them . . . Bernard's soul was flooded with such powerful grace, that while he gave himself completely to the work in hand his mind was completely taken up with God. . . . So while he worked, his prayer and holy thoughts went on uninterrupted, and however distasteful the work may have been it made no difference to his love and devotion.

Whatever of value is found in the Scriptures, whatever was spiritually inspiring, he confessed to have received above all in meditation and prayer, especially in the woods and the fields. To his friends he used to say in his own joyful, humorous way: "For all this I had no other formators than the oaks and the beech trees."

During the hours that were not devoted to manual work, he either read, or prayed, or meditated. If he had a chance to be alone he would use it for prayer; but since true solitude is something of the heart, it hardly mattered whether he was by himself or surrounded by many others.

It was his great delight to pass hours in reading Scripture. He used to read the books straight through in their proper order, and never had any difficulty in understanding what the words meant. He used to tell that he found it easier to understand the text of Scripture itself than lengthy explanations of it. Even so he did read the old commentaries of the Fathers. . . . Like them he drank avidly of the one fountain which is Holy Writ, and was filled with the same Spirit who inspired these writers.

As regards Bernard's own teaching, as it has come down to us in letters, sermons and treatises, they confirm what we learn from the *Vita Prima*. The first example comes from a letter addressed to a candidate engrossed in learning, who found it hard to renounce his studies. Bernard replied:

> Believe me who have experience, you will find much more while laboring in the woods than you ever will among books. Woods and rocks will teach you what you will never hear from me. Do you perhaps imagine that you cannot suck honey from the rocks and oil from the hardest stone, that the mountains do not drip sweetness and the hills flow with milk and honey, that the valleys are not filled with corn? So many things occur to me which I could say to you that I can hardly restrain myself. But, as it is for prayer and not for a sermon that you have asked me, I will pray to God that with his laws and his commandments he may open your heart. Farewell! (Letter 107)

The spirit which animated Bernard's understanding of formation is revealed to us in two other letters, sent to console the parents of a Geoffrey of Péronne. While holding uncompromisingly the lofty ideal of the monastic call, Bernard could win over his correspondents by assuring them of the tender care and love which would accompany them in their pursuit of this sublime call. The first of these letters is addressed to Geoffrey of Péronne and his companions, a band of some thirty noble youths whom Bernard had converted during a visit to Flanders, where the Abbey of Dunes, in Belgium, near the coast of the British Channel, was flourishing. This first letter is destined to encourage them to persevere in their decision:

> I congratulate you, my dear sons, and myself also, for I have heard that I am deemed worthy to help you in your good purpose. I will do what I can to advise you and I promise to help you as much as I am able. If I seem necessary to you or at least if you deem me worthy, I shall not begrudge the trouble and I shall try not to fail you. If it is the will of heaven, I will earnestly take this burden on my shoulders, although they are already bowed with care. Joyfully and, as the saying goes, with open arms I will receive you as fellow citizens of the saints, servants of God's household. How gladly will I not, in the words of the Prophet, "bring out bread" to those who fly from the sword; water to those who thirst. (Letter 111)

The second is addressed to the parents of Geoffrey to console them:

> If God is making your son His own, as well as yours, so that he may become even richer, even more noble, even more distinguished and, what is better than all this, so that from being a sinner he may become a saint, what do either you or he lose? But he must prepare himself for the kingdom which has been prepared for him from the beginning of the world. He must spend the short time which remains of his life on earth with us in order to scrape off the filth of secular life and shake off the dust of the world, so as to be fit to enter the heavenly mansion.
>
> If you love him you will surely rejoice because he is going to the Father, and such a Father! It is true that he is going to God, but you are not losing him, on the contrary, through him you are gaining many sons. All of us at Clairvaux will receive him as a brother and you as our parents.
>
> Knowing that he is tender and delicate perhaps you are afraid for his health under the harshness of our life. But this is the sort of fear of which the Psalm speaks when it says: "There, they were brought in great fear, where no fear was." Have comfort, do not worry, I shall look after him like a father and he will be to me a son until the Father of mercies, the God of all consolation, shall receive him from my hands. Do not be sad about Geoffrey or shed any tears on his account, for he is going quickly to joy and not to sorrow. I will be for him both a mother and a father, both a brother and a sister. I will make the crooked path straight for him and the rough places smooth. I will temper and arrange all things that his soul may advance and his body not suffer. He will serve the Lord with joy and gladness, his song will be of the Lord, for great is the glory of the Lord. (Letter 112)

Some may be surprised that in all that we have said up to now about Bernard's understanding of monastic formation, nothing has been said of the liturgy, the Opus Dei, so prominent in the Benedictine Rule.

Saint Ephrem, the genial initiator of choral celebrations in the Church in the fourth century, who later exercised an all-pervading influence on their composition as well as on their performance, expected from monks a meditative disposition requiring much discipline:

> When you stand at prayer recollect your mind with passion.
> Put a bridle on your thoughts and keep them in your heart. Let
> not your body stand there and your mind be distracted by other
> affairs. Your body will be a church and your mind a glorious
> sanctuary. Let your mouth be the censer and your lips the in-
> cense. Let your tongue be the minister who pleases the Godhead.

We should not forget that Bernard has left us a quite remarkable
collection of sermons on the liturgical seasons and feasts of the
year. His concern for the performance of the liturgy appears even
in his *Sermons on the Song of Songs*. After sharing an exalted and
protracted meditation on the first verse of the second chapter:
"I am the flower of the field and the lily of the valley," which he
attributes to the Bridegroom, he suddenly turns to the liturgy.
And, while he is well aware of the weaknesses which affect the
performance of this monastic work, weaknesses of individuals
as well as of communities, he nevertheless expects from them all
a participation of such a high quality which even today, an age
of earnest liturgical renewal at both the scholarly and devotional
levels, makes us blush:

> By our Rule we must put nothing before the work of God.
> This is the title by which our Father Benedict chose to name
> the solemn praises offered to God in the church, that so our
> legislator might more clearly reveal how attentive he wanted
> us to be at the work.
>
>   So, dearest brothers, I exhort you to participate always in the
> divine praises correctly and vigorously, that you may stand be-
> fore God with as much enjoyment and reverence, not sluggish,
> not drowsy, not yawning, not sparing your voices, not leaving
> words half-said or skipping them, not speaking through the
> nose or with a stumbling stammering, in a weak and broken
> tone, but pronouncing the words of the Holy Spirit with be-
> coming manliness, resonance and affection, and correctly, that
> while you chant you ponder nothing but what you chant.
>
>   Nor do I mean that only vain and useless thoughts are to be
> avoided at that time and in that place. Even those necessary
> thoughts about necessary community matters which frequently
> importune the minds of those brothers who have official posi-
> tions, are to be avoided.

Furthermore, even those thoughts have to be left aside which come from listening to the Holy Spirit before psalmody begins. For example, as you sit in the cloister reading books or as you listen to my talk, as you do now, these are wholesome thoughts; but it is not all wholesome to reflect on them during the psalmody.

For, if at that time you neglect what you owe, the Holy Spirit is not pleased to accept anything offered that is not what you owe. May we always be able to do our will in accord with His will, as He inspires, by the grace and mercy of the Church's Bridegroom, our Lord Jesus Christ, who is blessed for ever. (*Sermons on the Song of Songs,* 47:8)

Indeed, here again we have a supremely eloquent interpretation of Saint Benedict's recommendation for the celebration of the Divine Office: "Let us take part in the psalmody in such a way that our minds are in harmony with our voices" (chap. 19).

For this we would dare to say that what stands out most remarkably in the *Vita Prima* and in Bernard's own writings concerning monastic formation is the importance and the quality of community life, with its alternation of prayer, work and *lectio divina.*

Today, however, the "rediscovery" of the documents of the origins of the Order and of the authentic monastic writings of Saint Bernard and the other Cistercian Fathers who emulated him, coincides with the astounding development of communication media. This phenomenon, of which no one could have dreamt a century ago, put the accent on scholarly formation with the help and on the basis of academic studies.

In fact, in our modern or postmodern civilization, there is a subtle temptation hidden in this enterprise. When academic studies are pursued for their own sake, they can deter us from our call. A similar temptation threatens every voracious reader of these spiritual writings, even if they are Cistercian publications. Academic studies or pursuits cannot take the place of *lectio divina,* which demands from us an actualization of what we read in our own lives. What we read should be lived. It is this monastic quest, the monastic charism, and not literary achievements, however brilliant, which is required from monks if they are to make their contribution to the Economy of Salvation.

The purpose of *lectio divina* is to germinate in us seeds of conversion and to nourish spiritual aspirations. Candidates who come to us in Kerala are usually late vocations. The young ones are all drawn to priesthood, either diocesan or religious, after leaving high school or completing graduation. All have been brought up in deeply religious families whose faith has long been nourished by the conventional Latin devotions imported by the missionaries. They came to know the liturgical and biblical renewals, which started in the West at the beginning of the twentieth century, only years after the Second Vatican Council. They do not possess the variety of seeds which will germinate and make to flower a monastic or Cistercian charism. Our seniors continue to feed on their traditional devotions.

In order to obtain a change, a first, basic and delicate inculturation is required. This can only be slow and must be cultivated with discernment. At Kurisumala the first seeds of the monastic charism to germinate have come from the Bible and the liturgy. The latter also introduces us to the Fathers whose feasts we celebrate. The *Vita Prima* of Saint Bernard has proved to be inspiring, as well as some of his sermons. But the treatises are still an unexplored land to be discovered. The recently beatified saints of the Order bear little witness to the twelfth-century patrimony.

As Jesus Himself said to busy Martha, who complained of her sister's sitting at the feet of the Master to listen to Him: "Martha, Martha, you are worried and distracted by many things. There is need of one thing only. Mary has chosen the better part, which will not be taken away from her" (Luke 10:41-42).

The Cistercian Fathers have interpreted this pericope as an exemplary presentation of their own life, a life well-balanced on account of a healthy alternation of Martha's works and Mary's contemplation, nourished by a true *lectio divina* with its traditional steps of *lectio, meditatio, oratio, contemplatio!*

Saint Aelred, disciple of Saint Bernard and abbot of Rievaulx in Yorkshire, interprets this pericope as an allegory of the intimate union of two lives:

See, my brothers, if Mary were alone in the house, no one
would provide food for the Lord. If Martha were alone, no one
would enjoy His presence and His words. Martha represents,
therefore, action, the work accomplished by Christ; Mary, the
repose which frees us from corporal works to make us taste the
sweetness of God in reading, prayer and contemplation. . . .

Thus, brethren, during this life of misery and labors, Martha
must necessarily dwell in our house. Our soul must apply itself
to bodily works. As long as we have to eat and to drink, we shall
have to mortify our flesh by vigils, fasts, work. Such is Martha's
part. But Mary, that is spiritual activity, must also be present.
For we must not apply ourselves unceasingly to corporal exercises, we must also rest at times and taste how sweet the Lord
is. (Quoted from Charles Dumont, "Saint Aelred: The Balanced
Life of the Monk," *Monastic Studies*, No. 1, Pentecost 1963)

This healthy balance of Cistercian community life, its diversity
in unity, is still more impressively expressed in the allegory of
the *paradisus claustralis*, in which the unity of the community is
described as enriched by the diversity in which every monk has
his own saintly charism. Already quoted it earlier, it is worth-
while giving it here again as a fitting finale for our guidebook:

The monastery is truly a paradise,
a region fortified with the rampart of discipline.
It is a glorious thing
to have men living together in the same house,
following the same way of life.
How good and pleasant it is when brothers live in unity.

You will see one of them weeping for his sins,
another rejoicing in the praise of God,
another tending the needs of all,
and another giving instruction to the rest.
Here is one who is at prayer,
another at reading.
Here is one who is compassionate,
and another who inflicts penalties for sins.
This one is aflame with love,
and that one is valiant in humility.

This one remains humble when everything goes well
and the other one does not lose his nerve in difficulties.
This one works very hard in active tasks,
while the other finds quiet in contemplation.

Appendix

THE *HISTORY OF THE MONKS IN EGYPT*

"Those through whom the world is kept in being"

As the twelfth century of medieval Europe has been called the century of the Cistercians, we could also say that the fourth century of Christianity was the century of monasticism on account of the spectacular upsurge of monastic life simultaneously in the whole of the then-Christian world, and especially in the Egypt of the Desert Fathers. Their impact on Christianity has been beautifully described by Sister Benedicta Ward, SLG, in her introduction to the translation of the *History of the Monks in Egypt*, published jointly by Mowbray, Oxford, and Cistercian Publications, USA, under the title *The Lives of the Desert Fathers*. The first section opens with a letter of Saint Jerome (+ 420) to his friend Rufinus:

> I hear that you are penetrating the hidden places of Egypt, visiting the bands of monks and going around heaven's family on earth . . . at last the full weight of truth has burst upon me: Rufinus is in Nitria and has reached the Blessed Macarius.

Rufinus himself records this visit in Egypt with nostalgia:

> When we were drawing near this place, the monks were aware that foreign brethren were approaching, and at once they came out of their cells like a swarm of bees. With joyful speed and glad haste they ran to meet us.

And at the last stage of the journey in Scetis, he wrote: "This is the utter desert where each monk remains alone in his cell . . . There is a huge silence and a great quiet there."

The "huge silence and great quiet" of the desert was frequently invaded in the fourth century by such visitors. Basil the Great came after his baptism, Paula and Melania—the noble ladies from Rome—Egeria from Spain, Jerome from Bethlehem, Palladius from Galatia, Cassian and Germanus also from Bethlehem. It is from their accounts that a living picture of the Desert Fathers' lives can be formed. It is a picture, of course, painted by outsiders, based on what they observed and on what they were told, but all of them were remarkable personalities of their time. *Anachoresis*, the monastic life, was in the air and rumor of it spread throughout the Christian world.

It was not an easy journey into Egypt. And when John of Lycopolis congratulated the travelers, with a certain humor, on their determination to visit the desert, there is a note of real admiration behind it:

> What remarkable thing did you expect to find, my dearest children, that you have undertaken such a long journey, with so much labor, in your desire to visit some poor men who possess nothing worth seeing or admiring? . . . I marvel at your zeal, how taking no account of so many dangers, you have come to us to be edified, while we from laziness do not even wish to come out of our cave.

They had come, said the visitors, in order to learn about monastic life from the Egyptian monks, and they were to do so partly by conversation but even more by observation: "We have come from Jerusalem for the good of our souls, so that what we have heard with our ears we may perceive with our eyes." While John had spoken of himself and his colleagues "as poor and simple men who possess nothing worth seeing," the visitors describe them as:

> True servants of God . . . while dwelling on earth. . . . There was no town or village in Egypt which was not surrounded by hermitages, and the people depended on their prayers as if on God Himself. . . . It is clear to all who dwell there that through them the world was kept in being and that through them human life was preserved and honored by God.

When the monk defines himself, it is as a sinner, a weak man, not a strong one. The idea of the monk as one by whom human life is preserved and honored by God is, and must remain, an opinion from outsiders.

Alongside the definition of the monk as a champion in spiritual warfare, there are many indications of the very practical place the monk held in the life of society. There are stories of gardens of vegetables for the use of the monks and their visitors, of green plants growing which were never there before, of peasant farming in a rich soil, of gardens of trees, of flourishing agricultural projects. Sarapion organized a regular trade between the Faygum and the city of Alexandria on a large scale, sending wheat and clothing down to the poor of the big cosmopolitan city. The reason given was that there were no poor near the monasteries: "From the labor of the brethren they dispatch whole shiploads of wheat and clothing to Alexandria for the poor, because it is rare for anyone in need to be found living near the monasteries."

In Europe, in the Middle Ages, a conventional picture displayed three parts of society: those who fight, those who labor and those who pray, all contributing in different ways to the life of the kingdom. Prayer was a great action to be fulfilled in the body politic; the monks were like trees purifying the atmosphere by their presence. The monks are presented as the defenders and guardians of world peace, constantly keeping watch on the frontiers, armed against the demons for the sake of humankind.

The Role of the Monks in the Church and in the World

Saint Bernard had a similar understanding of the function of the monks in the Church. He even taught that their charism was meant to benefit the whole human race: "He sometimes reminded his monks of this in a humorous way during his familiar talks, when he used parables and comparisons of which he explained the significance." For example, when enumerating the various roles of the teeth of human beings, he applied this to monks: "They chew for the benefit of the whole body since they have been established to pray for the entire body of the Church, that is, all its members, living and dead."

Elsewhere, developing also with humor and fantasy the symbolism of the organs of the human body in order to show the bond which unites all the members of the Church, he comes to the stomach. It is not highly honored, and yet it is this organ that collects the food, nourishes the body, assimilates the food and sends out the juices necessary for life to the other superior and inferior members. Such are monks and hermits:

> They are the ones who sustain the Church: they are prefigured by Moses praying on the mountain, by Samuel spending the night in the shrine of Shiloh and by Elijah sojourning in the desert. They send forth spiritual juices to all: to the prelates as well as their subjects. Applying this to them we can say: "The human race subsists on account of a few; if they did not exist, the world would perish by lightning or an earthquake."[1]

The most usual way for the monks to live was in a small self-built cell, made of bricks of mud dried in the sun and mortar, with one or possibly two rooms. Besides these simple two-room cells, grouped loosely together, there were also monasteries, more permanent buildings for groups of monks in the district. The seven pilgrims visited a monastery built on the pattern of the cenobitic community of Saint Pachomius at Tabennisi, in which there was a large building to house all the monks, with a common refectory and a church.

The monks regulated and controlled the need for sleep by night vigils. The writer in the prologue says: "They kept watch waiting for Christ like loyal sons waiting for their father." To the discipline of sleep and food they added manual work, mostly agricultural, of necessity. There was the daily fight for existence for those who chose to live away from the settled lands near the fertile Nile. There is little mention of study or of the work of reading or copying books, except in the case of Evagrius, the

---

1. J. Leclercq, "Saint Bernard and the Contemplative Community," *CSQ* 7 (1972), 99–100.

most learned of monks. But they clearly had a basic reverence
for the study of the Scriptures. The monks chanted the Psalms
unceasingly as the basis of their prayers and canticles. In some
monasteries the Eucharist was celebrated daily:

> Monks, if possible, should communicate daily in the Mysteries
> of Christ . . . It is therefore useful for monks . . . to be ready
> every day, and to prepare themselves in such a way at any
> time, because it is thus that we are also granted the forgive-
> ness of sins.

Yet the most common practice reported in other early documents
is of the Saturday night vigil ending on Sunday morning with
the Eucharist.

As for the ideals and insights of monastic Egypt, that struck
our pilgrims during their conversations with the monks, they
noted their discourses on the great virtues of the desert—humility, discretion, realism, the single eye of a life for God. Yet John
of Lycopolis also dealt austerely with his visitors:

> Do not imagine that you have done enough. . . . Do not trust
> in yourselves. . . . Be careful . . . that you do not practise your
> virtues out of vainglory.

These instructions are usually framed in stories. But the essential
beginning is in repentance, compunction, the piercing of the heart
by sorrow, the need to leave all attachments, what is binding and
constraining. The desert is the place to acquire freedom.

The essential realism of conflict with the self and the truth,
however, could be another way of building up the ego unless
there is genuine asceticism of the heart, in the context of love and
friendship as essential parts of the monastic ideal, a universal
friendship that extended even to wild animals.

John describes the rooted selfishness that coils around the heart
like a serpent, continually burrowing deeper and creating a false
and illusory self which is continually restless and unstable. It is
a self which we mistake for our real self. It is precious to us and
we resist uprooting it. We cover it over with empty cheerfulness

or vain sadness. The restless heart is contrasted with the inner well of peace and stability, which is the work of the Spirit of God, whose presence produces those typical virtues of the desert— love, meekness, long-suffering, not judging others.

Apollo severely censured those who wore iron chains and let their hair become unkempt: "These make an exhibition of themselves," he said, "and chase after human approbation." It is only that which leads to the inner path of repentance that is recommended, and here there is agreement between this text and other literature of the desert.

As the prologue of the *History of the Monks in Egypt* says, the writer witnessed "their fervent love and great ascetic discipline," in that order. The place of the desert is presented as being per-manently the place of the cross: the monk will stand beside the Crucified with confidence, for the Crucified Lord became obedi-ent unto death.

Yet there is also in the *History of the Monks*, as in other desert literature, the other side of the cross, which is resurrection. The message of the monks is not their own worthlessness but the everlasting faithfulness of God. God, they say, does not tell lies and He is continually present with the monk, turning his sorrow into the joy of the Kingdom. The patriarch Jacob, to continue the image, wrestles with God in darkness and, permanently crippled as a result, he goes toward the brother he has betrayed and says to him: "Seeing your face is like seeing the face of God" (Gen 33:10). So there is in this text the image of the new Adam restored to heaven in the midst of his trials, not subsequent to them.

There are in the *History* images of light and joy, the life of the angels, sounds of heavenly mirth. The monks encountered are not gloomy men obsessed with their own asceticism; they are more alive and more approachable because of it. Even their physical appearance shows the new life that is within them. After forty years of solitude, John of Lycopolis is described as having a bright and smiling face. Bes is described as meek, gentle and utterly serene. Theon went out at night to give water to the wild animals. In Nitria, Ammonius welcomed those who came to the community with a feast:

Those who intended to live in the cells were invited to the church for a feast. And while they were still enjoying themselves, each brother filled his cloak or his basket with loaves or other suitable things from his own cell and brought them to the new ones, so that no one should know which gifts had been brought by which brother.

Another side of this life which comes from heaven is charity, and especially charity toward the brothers. The monks were renowned for the loving welcome they gave to guests, and there are instances in our *History* of such hospitality, from the prologue onwards. The most striking is the description of the reception given to the visitors in Nitria and Cellia, in the Latin version of Rufinus: "What can I say that would do justice to their humanity, their courtesy, and their love. . . . Nowhere have I seen love flourish so greatly, nowhere such quick compassion, such eager hospitality."

But visitors went away and charity to them was limited; what was permanent was the relationship among the monks. There are instances here of the care of the brothers for each other in need, even of the pleasure they might take in talking with each other, and above all there are instances of that great virtue of the common life, the refusal to pass judgment on others (see *The Sayings of the Desert Fathers*, Moses 2).

Another side of charity is found in the stories of the solitaries who return after many years to take part in the common life with the brothers. The desert is not presented as a place for misanthropes, eccentrics, individualists; it is rather, as the prologue says, "a place where they are separated in their cells but united in love." There is an unfussy charity among the monks and a dependence of each upon all.

Finally, there is another aspect of this life of hardship and happiness in pursuit of "the one thing necessary"; that is the idea of paradise. The orientation of the monks' life is toward heaven, toward the life of the other world. For this reason they are frequently referred to in this text as "angels," as living the angelic state. And in the prologue to the text, as already mentioned, the monks are said, "while dwelling on earth in this manner, [to] live as true citizens of heaven. . . . They are waiting in expectation of the coming of Christ."

Certainly there are stories of visitors who are also called "angels," who supply the monks with food, usually described as rare or exotic. The control of the appetite was never fully achieved. It is instructive to observe that gluttony—the first of the eight capital vices of Evagrius—was as much as sexuality, their continuous field of battle.

The single eye, and the heart at rest, is presented in this account as the end and purpose of the monk; perhaps the best summary is the description of Bes, who is presented as "having attained the angelic state," the summit of perfection:

> He lived a life of the utmost stillness, and his manner was serene. . . . He was extremely humble and held himself of no account. We pressed him strongly to speak a word of encouragement to us, but he consented to say only a little about meekness, and was reluctant to do even that.